The Orvis
Fly-Tying
Manual

The Orvis
Fly-Tying
Manual

TOM ROSENBAUER

PHOTOGRAPHS BY
TOM ROSENBAUER

The Lyons Press

Printed in the United States of America

9 8 7 6 5 4 3 2 1

Library of Congress Cataloging-in-Publication Data

Rosenbauer, Tom.
    Orvis fly-tying manual/Tom Rosenbauer.
        p. cm.
    ISBN 1-58574-202-3
    1. Fly-tying—Handbooks, manuals, etc.   I. Title.
    SH451.R62 2000
    688.7'124—dc21

                                                          00-060854

Contents

Introduction

I'D BE WILLING TO BET MY FIRST ATTEMPT AT FLY TYING was more pathetic than yours was or will be. I had sent away for a kit from Herter's 35 years ago. The only instructions in the kit were for a single pattern in the old *Noll Guide to Trout Flies,* and they were for the Fanwing Royal Coachman, one of the most difficult patterns in the history of fly tying. The book bore no resemblance to the materials in the kit: It was only by chance that all the materials for the Fanwing were in the box. I hacked my way through the fly, and, having read somewhere that dry flies had to be dipped in some kind of potion to make them float, promptly dipped the entire fly in head cement. This should have made the fly immortal, like an ancient insect preserved in amber, but I was so frustrated I threw it in the trash.

I have tried to remember what those early days were like so you don't begin in the same fashion. I don't think I've ever forgotten what it's like to be faced with a pile of strange materials and unusual tools, because I've taught fly tying all my adult life—at Trout Unlimited meetings, impromptu neighborhood "tie and lie sessions", and to coworkers at Orvis on lunch hours.

This book is excerpted from a larger book, *The Orvis Fly-Tying Guide.* That book includes instructions for eight additional patterns, an overview of most common fly-tying materials, hook charts, and pattern recipes for all the flies in the 2000 Orvis catalog. As I completed it I realized that a book with close to 1000 color photos, pushing the $50 price tag, would drive the price of a fly-tying kit beyond the reach of many would-be tiers, so we decided to create this smaller book and build a fly-tying kit around the book. Because the book and the kits were developed concurrently, you'll avoid the pitfalls of trying to learn fly tying by assembling your own materials, or by learning from a kit that does not have a proper manual.

All six of the patterns in this set are ones I carry in my fly boxes, all the time. They were selected for their fish-catching qualities, and because they demonstrate basic fly-tying skills that can be carried forward to thousands of other patterns. If you master these six patterns and start catching fish with your own flies, beware! This is an addiction for which there is no cure. You'll soon lust after a rolltop desk filled with feathers, furs, tinsel, and hooks.

1

Getting Started

A PLACE TO PARK IT

THE IDEAL PLACE TO TIE FLIES IS A ROOM OF YOUR OWN, an office or spare bedroom, with plenty of shelf space for books and materials. Natural light is wonderful for fly tying, so a big window at either side or behind you provides strong, color-corrected light. Make sure there is a door that can be closed tightly. Dubbing needles and scissors are sharp and attractive to small children, and both cats and dogs seem to prefer chewing on expensive hackle capes to anything else in your possession. You should have a broad, clean worktable and a chair that lets you sit hunched over a vise without back pain.

Barring this ideal location, you can use a temporary spot on a kitchen or dining room table if you are well organized and all of your gear is portable. In this case, get a pedestal vise and store all of your materials and tools in boxes that can be moved easily from one room to another.

There is no right height for a fly-tying vise. Some people like to look down on the fly and thus set the vise so that it is at chest level. I like mine higher, about chin level, but you should experiment to find the height that works best for your vision problems, if any, and your muscles. Adjusting the height is easier with a clamp vise as the jaws can be moved up or down on the stem. If you have a pedestal vise you'll have to find a table that brings the vise to a comfortable height. Your chair should be centered on the vise and it should be close enough to let you see every turn of thread in detail.

STORAGE

The best primary storage for all fly-tying materials is Ziploc® bags. They are perfect for any material that contains feathers, skin, or hair, because carpet beetles and moths can't get inside a sealed bag. Carpet beetles are the biggest destroyer of fly-tying materials. Learn to recognize these small insects by the red band in the middle of their bodies. If you find any in your fly-tying area, inspect anything that they might be into. If you find them (look also for sawdust-like material in the bottom of a bag, which means larvae have been chewing there), remove any bags that may have been infested. Throw them outside in the trash or open the bags, insert some mothballs or crystals, re-seal the bags tightly, and put them in the garage for a few months. Some of the materials may have been ruined, but you may be able to kill off the larvae before they ruin anything else. The bags might still have unhatched eggs in them, though, and should remain suspect as long as you keep them. Keeping the door to your tying room closed and making sure the window screens are tight will eliminate most problems before they start. However, sometimes bugs come in with material you have purchased. Tanned hides don't have bugs, but materials like wing quills and bucktails can't be tanned and may harbor bugs.

Even though bugs are not a problem with synthetics, tinsels, and other man-made materials, Ziploc bags still make great organizers because loose stuff stays put and you can keep like materials organized. Most materials already come in these bags, and you can then put smaller bagged materials inside bigger bags.

Plastic shoe boxes with tight lids make perfect storage devices. They stack, are usually clear, and keep bugs and pets out of your stuff. Label each box on three sides and on top with a waterproof marker—even stacked in a closet you'll always know where to find a white bucktail when you need it. Those drawers made for nails and screws are great for storing hooks, threads, tinsels, and other man-made materials but they are not so good for animal products because they aren't airtight. Big tackle boxes are also nice but they don't stack.

There is a portable tying bench on the market that opens up into a big storage area underneath. If you tie in various rooms in your house you can move your materials and work surface in a single trip.

Eventually you might want to invest in a big rolltop desk. They are great for fly tying, especially if you tie in an area that is used by the rest of the family. The top can be rolled down to keep your messy work area away from prying hands and paws, and you can stop in the middle of a bunch of flies and walk away without worrying.

LIGHTING

You need a lot of light to tie flies, and the older you get the more light you need. Trust me—strong lighting makes a huge difference in the quality of your flies. The best indoor setup is to have natural light from a window coming from one side and light from a strong lamp on the other. Of course this only works during the day and you will probably do a lot of your tying in the evening.

A portable light that duplicates the spectrum of natural light.

Your working light should come from overhead but angled slightly so the shadow from your hands working on the fly does not fall directly on the hook. The best lights available are ones with special bulbs that simulate the natural spectrum. You will be able to see the true outdoor colors of your flies and the lights are easier on your eyes. They are also supposed to improve your mood and combat Seasonal Affective Disorder—not uncommon when tying flies in the middle of February with a nasty case of spring fever. You can buy ones with adjustable necks from fly shops and catalogs.

The next best light is a draftsman's lamp that combines a fluorescent tube with an incandescent bulb. These are also a pretty close approximation of the natural spectrum.

Cheaper but not as good are high-intensity desk lamps. They don't give you the full spectrum of light but can be focused on the fly to give you good visibility.

Whatever lamp you buy, consider portability. If you don't have a fly-tying room chances are the light where you tie won't be right. And if you travel with your kit, count on motel rooms having the worst fly-tying light imaginable.

MAGNIFICATION

About ten years ago, the quality of my flies started slipping and I figured I had lost my touch or my concentration. I didn't realize I was losing my near vision with age and it took me a couple of years to figure it out, because I could read just fine. Fly tying requires top-notch close focusing, and if you can't manage naturally you'll need mechanical aids.

If you are under 35 years old you can probably skip this section. But for most of us, magnification of some type is as critical as good light. Even if you wear bifocals, the magnifiers in your glasses were designed for reading, not for attaching a Size 24 hackle to a thin wire hook with 10/0 thread. The maximum magnification you can get in standard reading glasses is about 3 diopters. Going to glasses with a 4 or even 5 diopter magnification improves the quality of your flies and lowers the frustration level.

You can get half glasses in this range in some fly shops and catalogs. You can also buy clip-on magnifiers that attach to regular prescription glasses. One of the best devices for improving your close-up vision is a visor that has magnifiers you can flip out of the way when not needed. The one I like has two levels of flip-down magnification plus a loupe for very close work. It even has tiny flashlights on each side of the head for directing a portable light source.

These flip-down magnifying visors offer three levels of magnification.

You may also see big magnifying loupes mounted on a flexible gooseneck. Adjusting to these can be difficult, though, and they tend to get in the way when winding materials around the hook.

There is another answer for those of you who are extremely nearsighted. I have been cursed with poor vision from birth and without glasses or contact lenses can barely negotiate my own living room. However, years ago I heard someone with the same vision problem talk about being blessed for fly tying. People who are nearsighted can focus at a very close distance, and this guy said he could tie the most incredible flies by taking off his contacts or glasses. I tried it. Without corrective lenses I focus at between three and four inches, like having built-in magnifiers. I don't tie like this in public because it looks pretty stupid, but when I'm home alone it looks like I am kissing Elk Hair Caddis.

CLAMPING THE HOOK

For most patterns, you should place the hook in the vise by clamping it at the bottom of the bend. This gives you more working room. With a spring tension vise, merely pull on the clamp until the jaws open up enough to accept the hook. Release the clamp and the hook will be secure. With a screw-adjustment vise, open the jaws enough to accept the hook and tighten the knurled knob firmly until it is hand-tight. With a cam-operated vise, it's a little trickier. Somewhere on the vise, either a knurled knob or a set screw on the stem pre-adjusts the jaw opening. Open the jaws enough to accept about 1½ times the diameter of the hook wire and squeeze the cam. The cam should move to a fully closed position with some resistance and not snap back. If it won't close fully under hand pressure, remove the hook and open the jaws a small amount. If the cam closes fully but the hook wiggles up and down in the vise when you pull on it, remove the hook and tighten the jaws a hair. A well-designed vise will hold a hook so well that you can bend the hook without moving it.

It's important to place the hook properly in the jaws. If the hook is too far back into the jaws you will have trouble closing them and the jaws can even snap under pressure. If the hook is too close to the narrow end of the jaws it can be shot out of the jaws like a bullet, with dangerous consequences. With most vises, the hook should be set about ¼ inch into the jaws for hooks bigger than Size 6 and half that for hooks down to Size 16. For the smallest hooks it's safe to place them almost to the end of the jaws and you'll get more working room.

THREADING THE BOBBIN

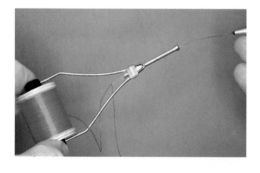

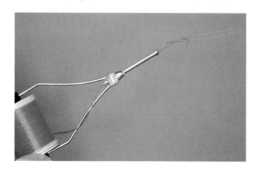

1. Run a bobbin threader through the tube until the wire loop pokes out of the end of the tube closest to the spool of thread. If the thread is frayed, snip it clean with scissors so it is easier to thread. Pull about six inches of thread from the spool and poke the end through the bobbin threader wire.

2. Pull the bobbin threader back through the tube. If your bobbin tube is not coated with wax, you can also just poke the thread into the tube and suck it back through.

   Check the tension on the legs of the bobbin. You should be able to feed thread from the spool by just pulling on the bobbin as you wind around the hook. It should be tight enough to provide moderate tension.

3. If the tension is too loose, remove the thread spool from the bobbin and bend the legs of the bobbin inward.

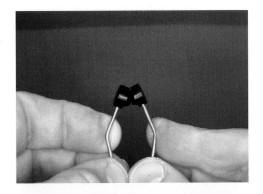

4. If it's too tight, spread the legs.

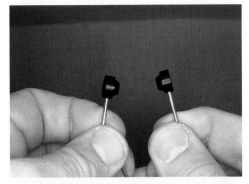

ATTACHING THREAD TO A HOOK

1. Assuming you are right-handed, pull six inches of thread from the bobbin and cross the thread in front of the near side of the hook, holding the bobbin in your right hand above the hook and holding the loose end of the thread in your left hand.

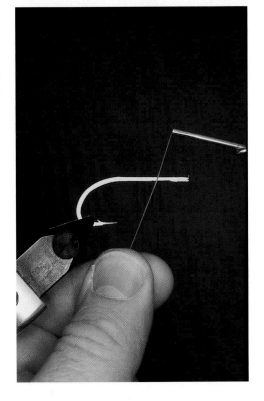

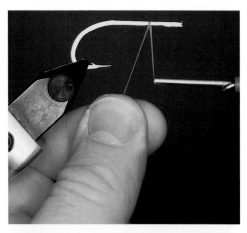

2. Bring the bobbin over the top of the hook and around the far side to the bottom of the hook.

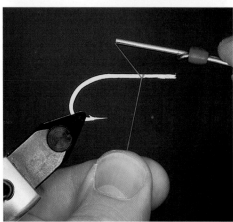

3. By pushing the bobbin to the left and the loose thread in your left hand to the right, wind the thread from the bobbin one wrap over the loose thread.

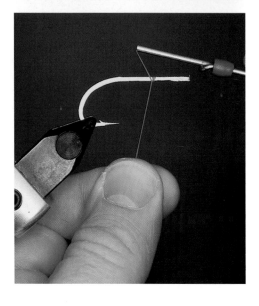

4. Make four more wraps over the loose end of the thread. Keep pushing your left hand to the right and your right hand to the left. Keep tension on both ends and work the thread coming from the bobbin a little more to the right with each turn of thread. You should now be able to release the loose thread in your left hand and put pressure on the thread coming from the bobbin without the thread slipping off the hook. If it slips, start over with more tension and make a few more wraps.

5. Using the loose thread and the shank of the hook as a guide, snip the loose end of the thread close to the hook. If you use both of these as guides you won't accidentally cut the thread going to the bobbin. Pull on the bobbin enough to feed thread from the spool. The thread should be secure and not unwind or spin around the hook. If it does, unwrap and start again.

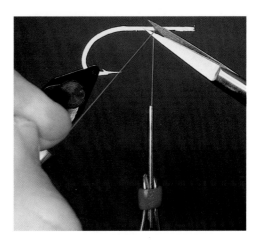

WINDING THE THREAD

For most operations, this bobbin is too far from the hook and you'll lose control.

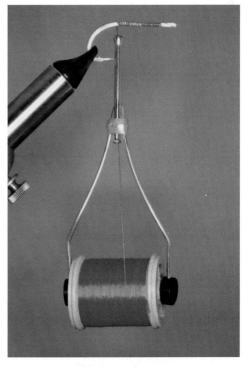

This bobbin is too close to the hook. The tube will get caught against the hook shank.

You should always wind away from you, as you did when starting the thread. Experiment with winding thread along the hook shank. Cradle the bobbin in your right hand, with your index finger just below the tube and your thumb on the spool. The bobbin tube merely rotates around the shank as you wind. For almost all tying, you should keep about one inch of distance between the end of the bobbin tube and the hook. When the tube gets too close, spin the spool with your thumb to release more thread. If you have to back up, just wind thread back on the spool by rolling your thumb in the opposite direction. If the bobbin tube is too close to the hook you'll have trouble maneuvering the bobbin; if it's too far away you'll lose control.

When you get close to the point of the hook, you'll have to weave in and out to keep the thread from catching on the point and getting nicked. Even though you are weaving, still guide the thread in one direction only—either toward or away from the bend.

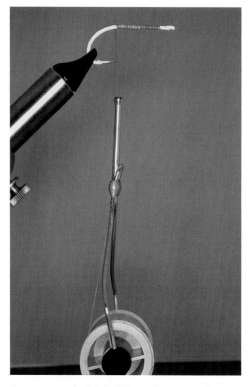

For most work, this bobbin is the correct distance from the hook.

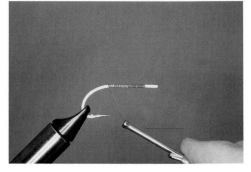

Weave the thread away from the hook point when winding close to the bend.

THREAD TENSION

Every turn of thread you take should be under tension. Think about each turn as you make it. Haphazard winds make sloppy flies that fall apart easily. When you are advancing the thread from one part of the shank to another you should be pulling at about half the breaking strength of the thread. When tying in materials, you may need to put almost 80 percent of the breaking strength into your winds. You get extra tension by locking your thumb on the spool.

A great exercise is to attach the thread to a hook, make a few winds, and pull on the bobbin, locking the spool with your thumb, until the thread breaks. Clean the thread off the hook and try it again. After repeating this a few times you'll have a great idea as to how much tension you can use.

TWISTING AND FLATTENING THREAD

Most fly-tying thread comes wrapped around the spool with a moderate twist. To be honest with you, for most tying I never worry about the twist in the thread, perhaps because I use the finest thread I can get away with. However, the twists in the thread can be manipulated for certain steps that make tying neater and easier.

When you don't want any bulk on the hook shank, as when binding down materials that will be covered by tinsel or floss, you can unwind or flatten the thread by giving your bobbin a good counterclockwise spin (if looking down on the bobbin from above). You see the twists go out of the thread and it will flatten close to the hook shank. Flatten thread for smooth underbodies, for binding down bulky materials, and for a smooth head on a steamer or saltwater fly. You may have to untwist thread in several steps if you are winding over a large hook.

Twisted thread adds bulk and gives you very precise placement of materials. Spin the bobbin in a clockwise direction until the thread twists into a tiny rope. Use twisted thread for building up bulk when raising dry-fly wings upright, when tying in loose materials like hair, or when placing tails at the bend of the hook.

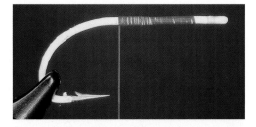

The thread at the front of this hook (closest to the eye) has been flattened. It does not add as much bulk to the shank. The thread wraps closest to the bend have been twisted, which gives more precise placement of materials.

ATTACHING MATERIALS TO THE HOOK

Attaching materials to the hook requires precise tension. More than anything else, thread tension distinguishes an experienced from an advanced tier, and like all things that are worth the trouble, it takes practice. You may watch a professional tier wind around the hook so fast the bobbin blurs, but you can bet that each turn of the thread he or she is taking has carefully controlled tension.

Almost all materials are attached to the upper side of the hook shank so most techniques work to force the material to stay on top of the hook. This is not easy when your thread is rolling around to the far side. Don't ever just "Tie something to the hook". It will end up everyplace except where you want it.

The Finger on Far Side

This technique is the easiest. It is used for materials that are neither stiff nor consist of a loose bundle of material. Tying yarn, chenille, floss, tinsel, and other body materials to the hook are typical places you can use this technique.

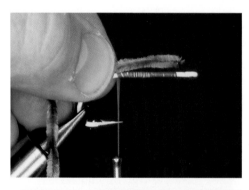

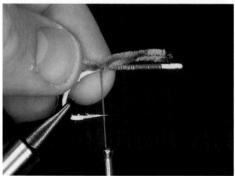

1. Start by placing the material you want to attach directly on top of the shank, or perhaps just slightly to the near upper side. Both ends of the material should lie parallel to the shank. Your thumb and forefinger should be holding the material right at the tie-in point, with your forefinger rolled slightly to the far side of the hook.

2. Loosen your thumb and forefinger slightly and bring a loose loop of thread over the top of the material and around the hook. No tension should be on the thread. When the bobbin is directly below the hook, pull straight down while pinching your forefinger tightly to the far side of the hook. Loosen up tension slightly and repeat the process three times, putting more tension on each successive wrap. In general, when at-

taching materials, you apply just friction tension on ¾ of the wrap and only apply firm tension in one direction. For placing materials on top of the hook, the normal scenario, pressure can be applied either straight up or straight down. When you want materials to lie along either side of the shank, as when making split tails, you apply pressure horizontally.

3. After three wraps in the same spot, advance the thread along the shank of the hook, always working away from the tie-in point. If you wrap back over the tie-in point you add sloppy bulk and take the chance of moving the piece you so carefully placed on top of the hook. After the initial wraps, you should not be putting any turn of thread on top of another, except for a slight overlap in winds. This is a critical process in fly tying and is one of the most difficult concepts for beginners to grasp.

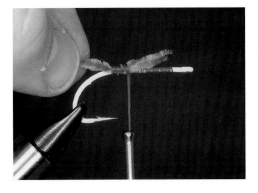

The 45° Roll

This is the best way to attach stiffer materials, like hackle stems, tails, and synthetic materials like vinyl ribbing.

1. Start with the material on top of the hook shank, with the material to be bound in at a 45° horizontal angle. The end of the material to be bound under should be pointing toward you and to the right. The end of the material that will not be bound under should face away from you.

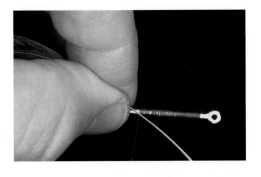

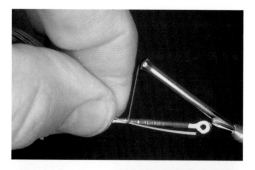

2. Bring the thread loosely over the top of the material, gradually rotating it so that it is parallel to the shank of the hook. Put some moderate tension on the material in a downward direction after the bobbin is under the hook.

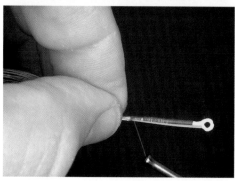

3. In subsequent turns, advance the thread toward the right with each wrap. Unlike the last method, no wraps should overlap so the foundation formed by the bound-in material is very smooth.

The Pinch

This is the best way to attach materials that consist of a bundle of fibers—hair, feather fibers, or wing quills.

1. Place the material directly on top of the shank, pinching it with the tips of your thumb and forefinger directly over the tie-in spot. It's usually best to spin the thread into a tight rope for the first part of this method, to ensure that you get precise placement of the thread.

2. Rock your thumb and forefinger slightly so that pressure is on the first knuckle. This opens up a spot over the tie-in place but still keeps the material in place. Keep pressure on the sides of the hook shank.

3. Take one loose turn of thread over the tie-in spot. Gently work the thread back into the space between your thumb and forefinger. Bring the thread all the way around the hook to a point directly underneath the tie-in spot. Rock your fingers back over the tie-in spot so that the thread you have just wound is covered up and pinched between your fingertips. Pinch the

thread and the material together, still keeping pressure on the sides of the shank. Pull the thread straight down with very firm tension, about 80% of its breaking strength. You can also experiment with bringing the thread over the top of the material, under the hook, and back up again, tightening with an upward instead of downward pull. Just don't tighten horizontally unless you want the material bound to the sides of the shank. Open up your fingers and take another wrap, pulling straight down in the same manner. Repeat once or twice more for a total of three to four wraps. Ensure that the material has not rolled to the far side. If it has, try to roll it back in place with your fingers, or unwrap and start over.

Now untwist the thread and bind the material under with smooth wraps, moving away from the part of the material that you do not want bound to the hook. If you have to start over, it's best to cut a new piece of material, as you will have already put a permanent crimp in it.

The Gravity Drop with Upward Pull

This method is mainly used to attach wide, flat, delicate materials on top of the hook: wing cases and shellbacks on nymphs, and grasshopper and caddis quill wings. It keeps them flat on top of the hook without crushing the fibers together.

1. Place the flat material directly on top of the shank. Push your index finger down on the material at the tie-in point.

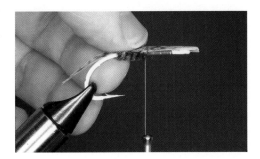

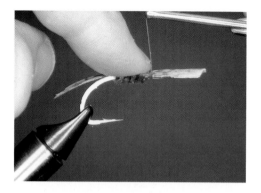

2. Rock back slightly on your index finger and place a loose loop of thread over the material. Bring the bobbin around and back down below the shank and just let it drop of its own accord while pinching your index finger down at the tie-in point. Make another wrap in the same fashion. Make a third wrap and then pull the bobbin up above the tie-in point.

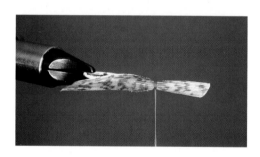

3. (Top view). Start advancing the thread down over the part of the material you will be binding under, using an upward pull for the next couple of turns and then returning to a standard downward pull as you get farther away from the tie-in point.

WINDING MATERIALS AND TYING OFF

Winding materials around a hook comes almost instinctively and I'm always surprised how quickly beginning fly tiers grasp the concept of switching the material from one hand to the other. In contrast, many people have trouble tying off a material under the thread; instead they merely wrap thread up against the material to be secured rather than crossing it with the thread. Here are the basics:

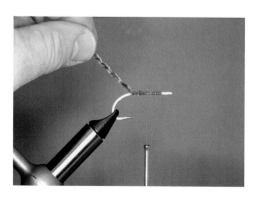

1. Begin by holding the material to be wrapped with your left hand. Wind it away from you, around the back side of the shank.

2. Underneath the hook, switch the material to your right hand.

3. Switch back quickly to your left hand and make another three-quarters of a revolution before using the right hand again.

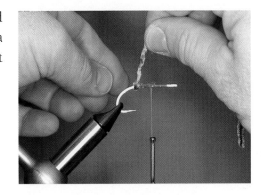

4. After you have made enough wraps and want to secure the material to the hook, hold the material above the hook with your right hand.

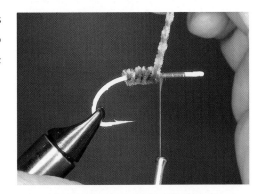

5. Use your left hand to push the bobbin over the top of the hook, making sure you cross over the material to be bound under.

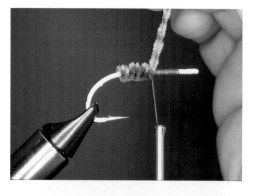

6. After the bobbin is three-quarters of the way around the shank, gently release it and let it fall under the shank so it hangs suspended by its weight. Now you can bring your left hand back to the near side to put downward pressure on the vise to help secure the material. Repeat the process at least three times or until the material is secure.

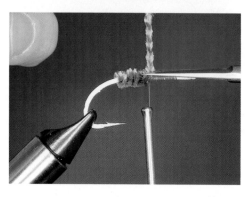

7. Let the bobbin hang below the shank and trim the material above the shank. This keeps you from accidentally cutting the thread.

THE WHIP FINISH

Half hitches are sometimes used, both in the middle of a pattern if you have to remove the hook from the vise to trim a hair body, or at the end of a fly when finishing the head. I don't recommend them. You can just as easily whip finish in the middle of a fly as you can tie half hitches, and a whip finish is neater and more secure.

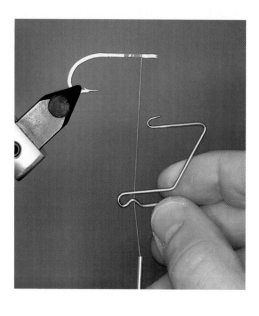

1. Start with three to four inches of thread hanging from the hook to the bobbin. Hold the whip finish tool in your right hand with your thumb on the near side of the handle, the lower loop of wire (the one with the notch) off to the left, and the open end of the hook at the top pointing to the right. Brace your index finger against the far side of the open loop, and brace your last three fingers on the far side of the handle. Hold the tool parallel to the thread, right against it, and raise the bobbin to a

horizontal position, pressing the notch of the lower loop against the thread. Don't let the tool rotate.

2. Catch the thread in the hook at the top by swiveling the top of the tool slightly to the left and then back. Keep tension on the bobbin so the thread does not slip out of the lower notch. Keep your fingers in place so the tool does not rotate.

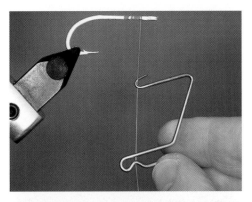

3. Move the bobbin up and toward the hook while releasing your forefinger. The upper end of the tool will rotate and flip sides. The most common problem at this point is keeping the thread secure on the hook and the slot. If you wait until the bobbin is higher than the tool to release your forefinger, you can keep better control.

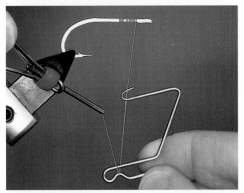

4. Keep moving the bobbin up and toward the hook while pulling the handle toward you.

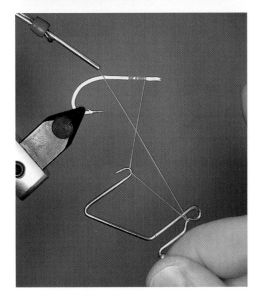

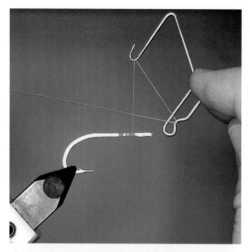

5. Bring the tool above the hook while letting it rotate freely. You'll notice there is now a place where the thread crosses itself on the far side, making a triangle.

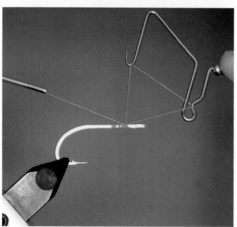

6. Move the lower left point of the triangle down to the tie-in point by keeping the tool stationary and moving the bobbin down and parallel to the hook shank. The point of the triangle should now be touching the fly at the point you want your whip finish to be placed.

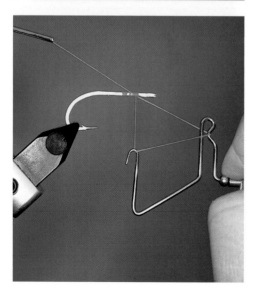

7. Hold the bobbin steady and rotate the tool smoothly around the eye of the hook. Make sure you clear the eye as the thread goes around. Repeat for five complete revolutions. Finish your last wrap under the hook.

8. Push the tool down and to the left while tilting the handle up.

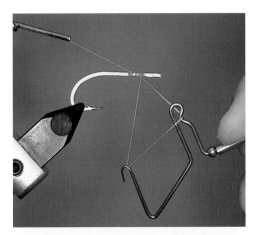

9. Keep pushing until the thread slips out of the lower notch.

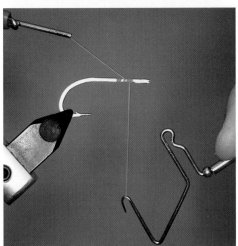

10. Pull up with the bobbin. Follow the thread up with the hook of the whip finish tool.

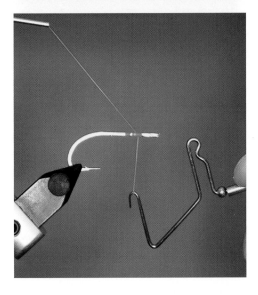

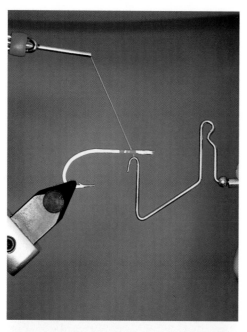

11. Keep pulling until the whip finish hook is trapped against the shank.

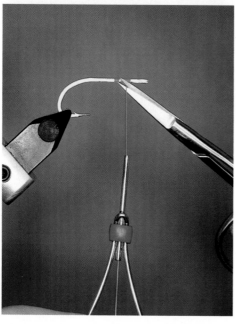

12. Slip the hook out of the loop and give a couple of short, firm pulls on your bobbin to secure the knot. Trim the thread carefully and your whip finish is complete.

WHAT TO DO IF THE THREAD BREAKS

Thread breaking in the middle of a fly, or getting cut on the hook point, is part of the game. Everybody does it. It's wise to have a pair of hackle pliers within reach even if you aren't winding hackle because they're an important part of reattaching thread.

1. If pre-waxed thread breaks, it won't unwind too fast so you have time to react.

2. Catch the loose end of thread still attached to the fly, clamp a pair of hackle pliers to it, and let it hang below the hook just like a bobbin. The weight of the hackle pliers will keep the thread in place while you get your bobbin re-threaded if necessary, as when the thread breaks it often slips out of the bobbin tube as well.

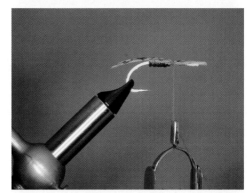

3. Re-thread your bobbin if necessary. Pull six inches of thread from the bobbin tube. Push the hackle pliers slightly to one side and start the new thread right on top of it, as if you were beginning on a bare shank.

4. Wrap the thread over itself five times. It should now be secure.

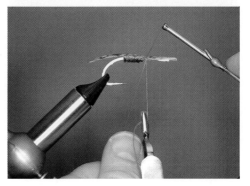

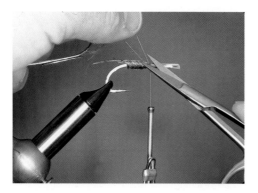

5. Pull both the broken thread and the tag end of the new wrap together on top of the shank. Carefully trim both. It's a good idea to put a small drop of head cement at this point before you continue the fly. You're back in business.

2

Tools

IT'S POSSIBLE TO TIE A FLY WITHOUT TOOLS. IT IS ALSO possible to ride a bicycle from Maine to California or climb Mount Everest without oxygen. I wouldn't advise you take on any of the above for fun. I once tied a bunch of hair-winged salmon flies in a dingy Nova Scotia motel room without a vise or bobbin. I held the hook in my left hand and manipulated materials with the thumb and forefinger of my right hand, while the other three fingers kept tension on the thread. The flies looked terrible and they didn't catch any salmon. Good tools are not very expensive and most will last for decades.

VISE

The vise holds the hook securely so that you can use both hands to manipulate thread and materials. Some will hold everything from a Size 28 midge to a Size 4/0 tarpon hook. Others specialize in either large or small hooks; some have removable jaws for different size ranges of hooks. Most advertising literature will tell you what size range a vise holds, but if it doesn't, assume the vise will hold at least size 4 through 20 hooks, which is the range of most trout flies.

Jaw Systems

The most common fly-tying vises use a cam-operated system, where a lever jams the jaws together around the hook. They all have adjustments so that you can change the opening between the jaws and the pressure applied when the cam is engaged. You should adjust the jaws so that when the cam is fully engaged the hook is held so firmly that it will bend before it will move in the jaws. If the hook slides up and down in the jaws, open the cam, tighten the jaws slightly and try again. If you have tightened the jaws so much that you have to force the cam, open the space between the jaws slightly. Forcing jaws, especially over a big saltwater hook, can snap the jaws.

Screw-tightened jaws are also available. With these, you simply tighten a big knob on the end of the jaws until it is hand-tight and the hook is held securely. The disadvantage with this type of vise is that you have to screw and unscrew the jaws every time you change hooks, even if they are all the same size.

Yet a third vise design uses an ingenious spring clamp that needs no adjustment, ever. You pull a lever to open the jaws against the spring tension enough to place the hook between the jaws, and when you release the lever the jaws spring closed around the hook. This vise is fast when tying lots of flies in different sizes and is popular with commercial tiers.

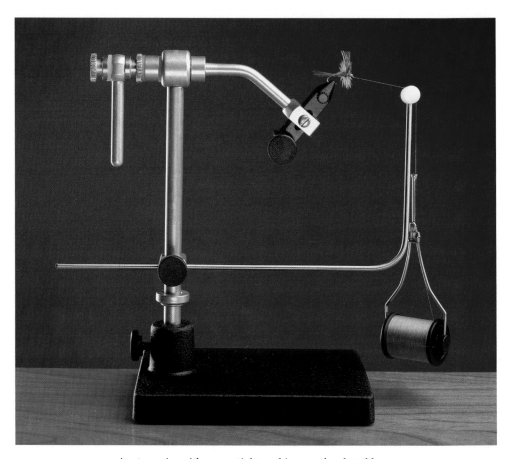

A rotary vise with screw-tightened jaws and pedestal base.

A vise with a spring clamp jaw system.

Clamp or Pedestal?

Vises must be secured to a table or other firm surface. One travel vise is built onto a metal ring that goes around a couple of fingers, allowing you to tie anywhere. Another actually comes with a special clamp for attaching to a car steering wheel. Neither of these is particularly handy, but if you are about to start on your coast-to-coast bicycle trip . . .

Most vises are made to attach to a table with either a C-clamp or a movable but weighty pedestal. Many vise designs can be attached either way, and you can usually buy the vise with one type of attachment and purchase the other later. C-clamps are very sturdy and are great if you tie fast or if you're tying a lot of big saltwater flies or deer-hair where a lot of pressure is put on the fly. However, if not used carefully they can mar the surface of a nice dining room table, and it is sometimes

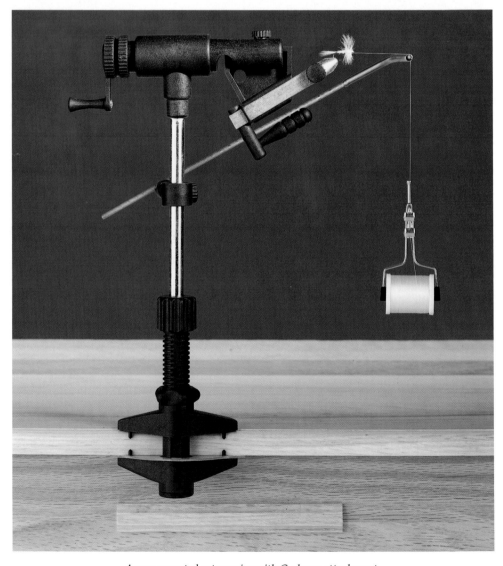

A cam-operated rotary vise with C-clamp attachment.

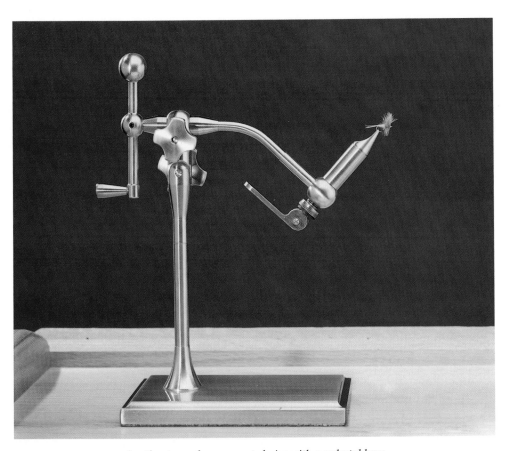

Another type of cam-operated vise with a pedestal base.

difficult to find a table with the right size edge for the clamp. Motel nightstands are notorious for not having a wide enough lip for a fly-tying vise.

With a pedestal, you can move your vise from one table to another in seconds, and you can tie on any surface, regardless of whether it has a lip or not. You can tie on a picnic bench, in your den, or on the kitchen table. The disadvantage of pedestal bases is that they are heavy if you take your stuff on a trip, and you are stuck with one jaw height above the table because the stem of the vise does not raise and lower as it does with a C-clamp vise.

Rotary or Not?

Vises can be made with stationary or rotary jaws. There is no advantage to stationary jaws other than cost, because a rotary vise can be made stationary by simply tightening the rotating feature down until it does not move. With a stationary vise, if you want to look at the bottom or far side of the fly, you must either remove the fly from the jaws and remount it upside-down, loosen the stem and flip the vise from right-handed to left-handed, or crane your neck around the far side of the vise. With a rotary vise, the jaws can rotate 360° without removing the hook from the jaws. A set screw controlled by a knob or allen wrench tightens or loosens the rotation of the jaws. By experimenting with this adjustment, you can come up with an amount of tension that keeps the vise stationary throughout most tying operations yet allows you to rotate the jaws and look at the far side or bottom of the fly (or to actually place materials at these hard-to-reach points).

There are certain operations in fly tying that lend themselves to true rotary tying as well. In rotary tying, the bobbin is placed out of the way, in a thread cradle. You grab the material you want to wind and rotate the jaws while feeding the material to the proper place on the hook. Not only is this faster, it lets you see where the material is going at every angle.

For example, let's say you are tying a fly where the entire hook shank needs to be covered with two layers of tinsel. In traditional winding, you bind one end of the tinsel in place, then wrap it around the hook by reaching over to the far side of the

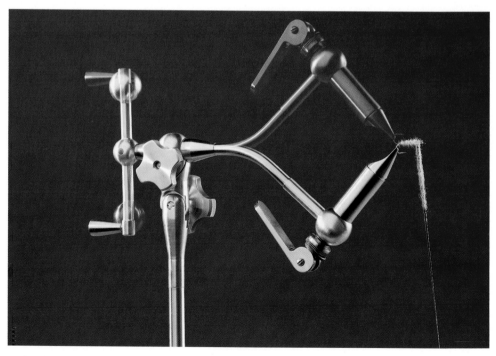

Tying with a rotary vise. The hook rotates with the vise jaws, but stays in the same horizontal plane.

hook with one hand, picking it up with the other hand, and then catching it again with the first hand. You can't just wrap the material around the hook with one hand because the bobbin gets in the way. Nor can you see how the material is laying down on the far side of the hook or underneath it.

With rotary tying, the bobbin is placed out of the way in a bobbin cradle and the tinsel is held in one hand while the other hand rotates the vise jaws. You can see exactly where each turn of tinsel is placed, eliminating any sloppy gaps or overlaps. When winding hackle, you also get smooth, even wraps. Some people find it an annoyance to switch from stationary to rotary tying, but if you tie lots of flies where much wrapping is necessary, rotary tying can be a fun and productive option.

Vise Recommendations

My recommendation is to get a C-clamp, stationary vise for your first vise. They are inexpensive, durable, and simple. You can get a decent one for under $50 and a great one around $100. If you want to upgrade, then advance to a pedestal, rotary vise. For this one you should expect to pay a minimum of $150 and as much as $400 for a beautiful machined tool with lots of adjustments, material clips, parachute tools, and other bells and whistles.

SCISSORS

Your scissors should be fine and sharp enough to cut a single hackle fiber or a few strands of marabou without pulling the fibers. Fine points are essential for precision work, where you need to clip off a hackle tip without cutting your thread or leaving too much waste sticking in the hook eye. You'll find straight blades more useful than curved. Finger handles should be wide and comfortable. Some tiers, particularly professional tiers, tie with the scissors around their fingers all the time, slipping the scissors up and down their fingers as needed. Don't feel bad if you can't get used to doing this—I have been tying for 35 years, some of that commercially, and I could never get used to keeping scissors on my fingers.

Most tiers like at least two pairs of scissors: One fine pair for delicate work and a heavier pair for cutting hair, tinsel, and large clumps of feathers like marabou. If you stick to one pair of scissors get fine-tipped ones and use the heavier inside edge for cutting hair and wire.

Tiny serrations on scissors help the blades grab materials and channel them into the blades. I feel they are an advantage even on fine-tipped scissors, and essential on heavier hair scissors.

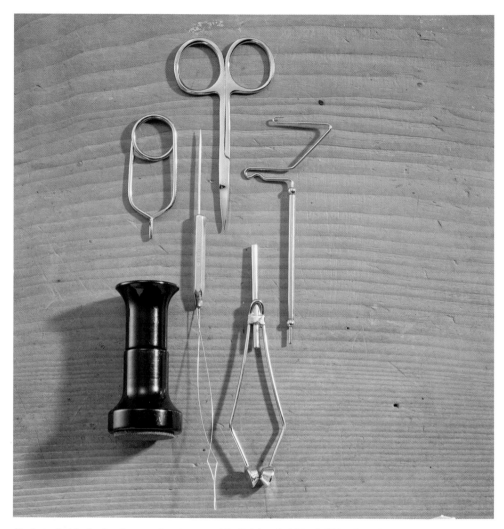

Basic tools (clockwise, from top): scissors, whip finisher, bobbin, bobbin threader, stacker, hackle pliers.

The best scissors are those sold by fly-tying shops and catalogs. I am a scissors freak and own over 20 pairs. I've bought expensive manicure scissors that cost three times as much as fly-tying scissors and they don't work as well. Fly tying scissors come from surgical supply manufacturers but suppliers modify these tools specifically for tying.

BOBBINS AND BOBBIN THREADERS

The best modern bobbins are made from a narrow tube attached to a set if wire legs, which hold the spool of thread or other material in place with plastic or metal balls or discs. The tube helps you place thread where stubby fingers won't go, and the bobbin itself holds the thread and keeps tension on the thread while you tie, and when both hands are free and preparing materials. Some of the tubes are polished metal, others are ceramic or metal lined with a ceramic insert, which will last a lifetime of tying. Those with flared ends don't plug up with wax as easily.

If you get a bobbin that cuts thread because of rough edges on the tube, send it back for a refund immediately. This never happens with the more expensive models but will occasionally happen with budget-priced bobbins that only cost a few bucks.

Because most of the threads we use today are pre-waxed, the bobbin tube gets plugged and it is not always possible to suck the thread through the tube. Get a bobbin threader, which is a simple piece of bent wire soldered to a nice handle. The wire is soft enough to prevent scoring the inside of the bobbin tube. If you're on a budget floss threaders work, too.

HACKLE PLIERS

Hackle pliers are used to hold hackles and other delicate materials, and to position them with an exactness not easily obtained with stubby fingers. They can also be used to spin dubbing on a loop or to temporarily hold thread if it breaks in the middle of a fly.

Hackle pliers are simple positive-locking clamps, where a squeeze to the sides opens the jaws and releasing them tightens the jaws over the material. They should hold a material firmly enough so it does not slip out under tension, without sharp edges that might cut the material

Basic hackle pliers, sometimes known as "English style", are the best all-around choice. The best ones have wide side plates that make the pliers easy to squeeze, and one side of the jaws is coated with soft plastic or rubber. This helps the pliers grip delicate feathers without cutting or breaking them.

A smaller pair of hackle pliers is handy for winding hackles smaller than Size 20, or for winding delicate feathers like peacock herl, single strands of ostrich, or pheasant tail fibers.

Most pliers have a wide loop at one end for slipping around your finger. This way, a hackle can be wound smoothly around the hook without having to let go of the pliers, except for a brief moment when you pass the pliers around the bobbin. Some tiers say you get better control by just holding the pliers by your thumb and forefinger and switching hands when winding around the hook but I think you can get equal control by placing the loop over a finger.

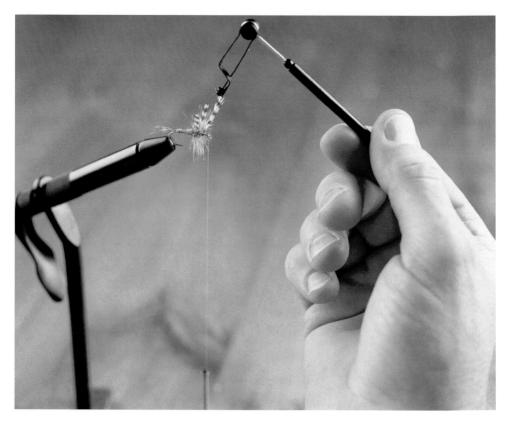

Rotary hackle pliers.

One special design consists of a tiny pair of hackle pliers attached to a stem that allows the pliers to rotate freely, both horizontally and vertically. They are great for all-purpose work and especially handy for tricky procedures like winding parachute hackles.

Large or long hackles can also be wound with your fingers. Big saltwater hackles and dry-fly saddle hackles longer than three inches can be handled nicely without pliers, but this may be limited by the dexterity you possess in your fingers.

DUBBING NEEDLE

A dubbing needle is simply a needle attached to a handle, preferably not a round one so that it does not roll off the table. I have a habit of involuntarily catching materials that fall of the table between my thighs, and have impaled myself more than once on a sharp dubbing needle! A dubbing needle is of course used to pick out dubbing to make it look fuzzier, and for folding wing cases on nymphs. It is also the way you apply head cement to the fly, either in the middle of the fly or after you have whip-finished the head. You can also use this tool to pick stray fibers out of the hook eye or to make minute adjustments to materials. Some people use the sharp point of their scissors for these procedures but scissors aren't as precise and sometimes the thread gets cut involuntarily.

WHIP FINISHER

A knot must be used to finish the fly so the head does not unwind. Some flies also require that you tie off the thread in the middle of a pattern, for example putting epoxy on the body of a fly before you put it back in the vise to attach a wing. Several half hitches are sometimes recommended. Don't even consider half hitches. They are bulky and are nowhere near as secure as a whip finish. The whip finish is a knot that winds the thread under itself about five turns—like the nail knot used to attach a leader to a fly line, or when you whip a thread under itself when winding a guide onto a rod.

Whip finishes can be done by hand or by a handy tool invented by Frank Matarelli. The tool makes a tighter, neater knot and it can place the knot in tricky places, like at the head of a tiny midge or under a parachute hackle. It is by far the hardest tool to use in fly tying; even so it can be mastered in a half-hour of diligent practice. Nothing seems to be more satisfying to a novice fly tier than to learn to use this tool, and once mastered, it's a crowd-pleaser for non-fly tiers to watch.

STACKER

This tool is used to level the ends of many kinds of hairs, so the fine ends line up flush before tying in. You can do this by hand by pulling small bunches out and repositioning them, but it takes a long time and the results are never as neat as with a stacker. The basic type consists of a brass tube with a stainless steel base. You place a bunch of hair in the end of the tube, fine ends first, and tap the stacker on the table. When you slide the tube out of the base the ends of the hairs will be perfectly even. Really neat ones have clear or open bases so you can see exactly when the hairs are lined up. For most flies the medium size is fine, but if you do a lot of work with big streamers you may want to get a large size to accommodate wide bunches of hair.

DUBBING SPINNER

For spinning fur on a loop, you can use your hackle pliers but a dubbing spinner is faster and more fun. The basic type consists of a pair of small hooks to catch the loop, plus either a heavy brass counterweight that you start spinning with your fingers and then let its momentum finish the spinning. Another fancier model mounts the counterweight on a shaft with ball bearings, and once the loop is spun you can use the shaft to wind the spun fur around the hook.

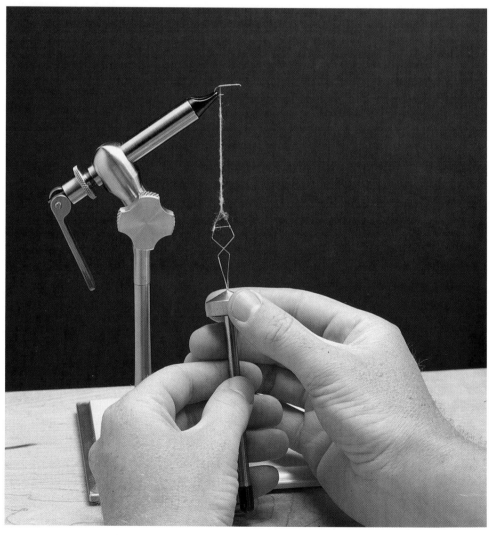

Dubbing spinners make looped dubbing an easy process. This one even has a ball-bearing shaft.

This rotating drier is battery-operated and portable.

ROTATING DRIER

If you tie epoxy flies or big streamers with glossy heads, this motorized tool gives the finished product a perfectly smooth finish. You place the flies in a piece of foam attached to a battery-operated motorized shaft on a slow governor and let them rotate from a few minutes to overnight, depending on how long it takes the cement to dry. Without this tool, you have to rotate the flies by hand or in a rotary vise as they are drying to keep the epoxy from running to one side, and the tool frees up your tying time.

HACKLE GAUGE

This is a tool with a small post that you fan a hackle around. It is marked with the correct hackle size for each hook size. I don't use this tool because I fan hackles around the hook as I am tying, but these gauges are very popular so I felt compelled to mention them.

HACKLE GUARDS

This is another tool I don't use but one that is popular. Hackle guards are cone-shaped pieces of metal or plastic that keep you from catching hackles in the thread when you finish the head of a fly. I think you can do just as good a job with your fingers, even on tiny flies.

TWEEZERS

These are almost essential but not quite. Tweezers or fine-tipped forceps should be fine enough to pluck a single hackle fiber that has gone astray. They are useful for picking up hooks or small materials. Mine are usually downstairs in the kitchen where they are used to remove ticks from pets and I don't miss them very much.

DUBBING TEASER

This can be anything from a piece of male Velcro glued to a pencil to a fine wire brush to a miniature plastic rake. They are used to brush dubbing under the thorax of a nymph or between the ribs on the abdomen of a fly. Slightly handier than a dubbing needle and fun to use—but not essential.

WING BURNERS

Elegant wings for dry flies can be made by placing a hackle feather inside a brass tool that is cut to the shape of a mayfly, caddisfly, or stonefly wing, then burning the outside of the feather away with a butane lighter. This can also be done with certain synthetic materials. The practice is not as common today as it was ten years ago but these tools do make gorgeous realistic wings.

DOUBLE-EDGE RAZOR BLADES

Use these to trim deer hair bodies. Carefully break in half and put some electrician's tape on the broken end to make it easier to hold. Also handy for scraping head cement off your dubbing needle. Single-edge blades are okay for scraping the dubbing needle but not sharp enough for trimming deer hair.

NEEDLE-NOSE PLIERS

Pliers are useful if you like barbless hooks, as you can debarb each fly as you tie it. They also come in handy for opening stuck bottles of head cement or caps on tubes of Super Glue.

POST-ITS AND PENCIL

Keep a Post-It pad handy for writing down materials you realize you need as you are tying. They are also great as disposable mixing areas for epoxy.

TRASHCAN

Make sure you have one unless you live alone. You can buy handy wire trash-bag frames that fit on the edge of a table right under your work area. I just use a plastic trash can on one side or the other and sometimes I actually hit it. Needless to say I keep a small hand vacuum cleaner close at hand.

PLASTIC STACKABLE BOXES

Plastic shoe boxes or the bigger styles are wonderful for storing materials. They are airtight enough to keep out beetles and moths and can be stacked in the corner of a room or in a closet. They keep out most cats and dogs but not ferrets. A heavy rubber band around the outside will discourage even ferrets, though.

LIGHTER

A lighter is essential if you burn wings or tie extended bodies with Vernille or Ultra Chenille, as you taper this material by singeing the ends.

TIPPET MATERIAL

You can make weed guards with heavier monofilament, and I like to use 4X tippet when I need a strong clear rib on a fly.

3

Woolly Bugger

THIS IS MOST FLY TIERS' FIRST ATTEMPT AND I'D ADVISE YOU not to buck the trend. I can teach someone who has never held a hook in his or her hand to tie a fishable Woolly Bugger in 45 minutes. Besides a somewhat sloppy head, it will look as good as one of mine. The other reason the Woolly Bugger is satisfying is that you can take one to your nearest bass lake, bluegill pond, trout stream, striper estuary, or bonefish flat and be tight to a fish in short order—assuming some willing fish and decent presentation. I've caught everything from steelhead to carp to sunfish to tarpon on this fly; it's probably the most universal fly for both fresh and salt water known to us today.

The Woolly Bugger was first tied in 1967 by Russell Blessing of Lancaster, Pennsylvania, who added a marabou tail to a Woolly Worm in an attempt to imitate a hellgrammite, the big, mean larva of a dobsonfly. I saw the fly about five years later on the upper Beaverkill. I was sitting on the edge of a deep pool with Ron Kusse, a bamboo rod maker who was running the old Leonard Rod Company at the time. It was one of those midday breaks in August when you realize you won't catch a fish for seven hours, when the sun leaves the water.

"Wanna see something amazing?" Ron asked. I cringed as he knotted this big ugly fly to his 38H Leonard bamboo and cast right across the pool. After letting the fly sink for a few seconds, he began stripping it back with about the same retrieve you'd use for barracuda. Four or five trout nailed that fly despite the bright sunlight and August heat and I was hooked as firmly as they were.

The way we fish Woolly Buggers today has little in common with the behavior of hellgrammites, which are poor swimmers. Although the fly is deadly fished on a dead-drift like a nymph, most of the time it is stripped actively, and probably looks more like a sculpin or crayfish to a trout or bass.

You can tie this fly in any color you want. I understand Blessing's original pattern had a peacock herl body and black ostrich tail; the classic version today uses olive chenille and black marabou, which are cheaper and more durable. Tom Piccolo's version for stripers, the Picabugger, is all chartreuse. Jim Finn's color scheme for northern Virginia trout streams, his "Golden Retriever" has a body of tan Estaz or Crystal Chenille and a tail of tan marabou. I've used a giant pink-and-white Bugger for salmon in Alaska and steelhead in the Lower 48.

Whatever colors you try, it's best to weight these flies, at least slightly, because the palmered hackle and fluffy marabou can float a streamer hook for the first few casts, until the fly gets wet. A terrific variation is adding either a brass bead or cone to the head of the fly before tying; the bead adds some sparkle and gets the fly down quickly.

In a pinch you can even slide a bead down the tippet in front of an unweighted fly, but you didn't hear it from me.

	MATERIAL	SUBSTITUTE
HOOK	4X Long Streamer, sizes 2 through 12.	3X Long Nymph.
WEIGHT	Non-toxic wire.	Brass or tungsten bead or cone slipped over hook and pushed up to eye.
THREAD	Black 6/0.	Red.
TAIL	Tip of black marabou feather.	Bunch of black ostrich herls. Either feather may also be used in white, yellow, tan, or chartreuse.
BODY	Olive chenille.	Peacock herl; or any other color of chenille to match tail.
HACKLE	Grizzly, palmered through the body	Black is most common alternate but almost any color can be and has been used.

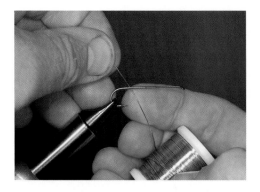

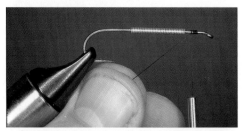

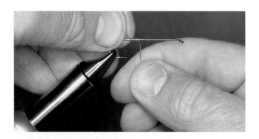

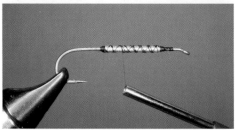

1. The non-toxic weighting wire should cover about one-half of the shank, leaving enough room to tie in materials at the tail and finishing the head without making a big lump. Holding a piece of wire, or the entire spool, in your right palm, hold on to the end of the wire with your left hand. Cross the wire behind the shank and wind it around the hook with your right hand.

2. Feed wire from your palms as you wind the wire in even turns. Don't worry if they aren't adjacent to each other as you can push the turns together with your fingernails as you wind.

3. Stop the wire when it is about one-sixth shank length behind the eye. Start your thread in front of the wire.

4. Wind back and forth just in front of the wire until a bump of thread the same diameter as the wire is built up. Wind the thread onto the wire, working toward the bend.

5. Select a marabou feather with even tips and lots of fuzz. For ease of handling, it should be at least twice the shank length.

6. Holding the marabou in your right fingertips, with the tip of the feather pointing toward the rear of the fly, hold it over the shank until about one shank length sticks out beyond your fingertips. Adjust your grip until it is the right length.

7. Grab the marabou with your right fingertips at a spot even with the end of your left fingertips.

8. Trim the butt of the marabou feather, leaving at least a half inch sticking beyond the end of your fingertips. Wet the part of the feather beyond your fingers—this makes it much easier to handle. Bring the thread back to the point where the shank ends and the bend starts. Make sure you come back far enough—if you don't the marabou will wrap around the bend when you cast and the fly won't swim properly. In the same light, don't wrap the thread back over the bend because the marabou will be tied in pointing down—it should come straight off the shank.

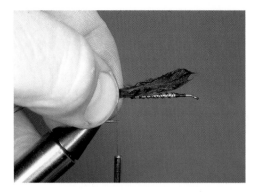

9. Attach the marabou to the spot where the thread was hanging with three Pinch Wraps: Hold it in place at the tie-in point with your left thumb and forefinger, bring the thread over the shank and around the far side while rocking your left thumb and forefinger back onto the first knuckle, slipping the thread in between them. Pinch them back over the marabou and tighten the thread by pulling straight down with the bobbin tube. The marabou should stay on top of the shank. If you pinch the sides of the hook tightly it should stay in place. Make two more tight pinch wraps.

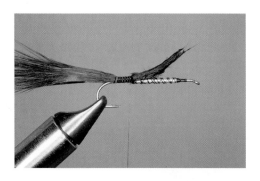

10. Wind the thread forward to the wire in smooth, tight, slightly overlapping wraps. Stop just short of the wire.

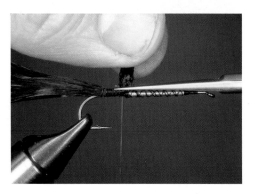

11. Trim the marabou by lifting it straight up and trimming with your scissors, using the shank as a guide. Wind a few turns of thread over the butts of the marabou, then wind the thread back to the bend—right at the spot you made the first wrap over the marabou.

12. Select a saddle hackle with a wide center web. The fibers on each side of the stem can be anywhere from one to two hook gaps in length. Strip the fuzzy down at the base of the feather by pinching it with your thumb and forefinger and pulling straight down toward the butt of the feather.

13. Grasp the saddle hackle by its tip and stroke the fibers back toward the butt with the fingers of your other hand.

14. Hold the feather just below the tip and carefully snip the hackle fibers from each side of the stem for about the top half inch of the feather. Stroke back any fibers that stick out over the tip and hide them under your fingertips.

15. Without releasing your grip, hold the trimmed tip of the feather against the near side of the hook and tie it in place with a 45° Roll. Make a half dozen very tight turns over the tip so it does not pull out when you begin wrapping it.

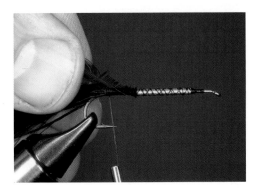

16. Wind forward to the edge of the wire and back to the bend to further secure the feather.

17. Cut a five-inch piece of chenille. Grab one end and remove the cotton fuzz with your fingertips, leaving the black threads at its core exposed.

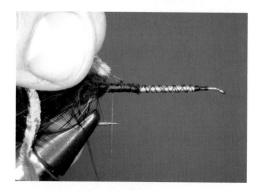

18. Tie the chenille in at the same spot you began wrapping the marabou and the hackle. Wind forward with tight wraps, covering the threads.

19. Advance the thread to a point just beyond the bump in front of the wire. Don't get too close to the eye—if you do, you'll end up with a bulky head and possibly waste material stuck in the eye. Twist the chenille between your fingertips four or five times—this makes it look better when it's wound.

20. Wind the chenille away from you, over the top of the shank with your right fingertips.

21. Catch it under the shank with your left fingertips while you bring your right hand around the bobbin.

22. Catch the chenille again with your right hand.

23. Continue wrapping the chenille forward in adjacent turns, so that each turn of chenille touches the preceding one but does not overlap. When you get to the spot where the thread is hanging, hold the chenille in your right hand while bringing the bobbin over the shank with your left. You'll have to let go of the bobbin on the far side, then grab the bobbin underneath the shank and pull down with firm pressure. Repeat the process about four wraps.

24. Trim the chenille on top of the hook, close to the shank.

25. Make about a half dozen wraps over the trimmed end of the chenille.

26. Grasp the saddle hackle that was left hanging at the bend of the hook. Pull it gently, straight up, and stroke the hackle fibers back until they all sweep back toward the tail. It may help to wet your fingertips.

27. Grasp the butt of the hackle in your fingertips or in a pair of hackle pliers. Wind the hackle forward in even spirals. You may have to twist the hackle to keep all of the fibers pointing back toward the bend, and you should stroke them back after each turn.

28. When you get to the point where the chenille was tied off, secure the hackle in the same manner. Make sure you take at least a half dozen turns—hackle is harder to secure than chenille.

29. Trim the tip of the hackle on top of the hook, close to the shank.

30. Stroke any hackle fibers that are not sweeping back toward the bend with your left fingertips and hold them in place while you take another half dozen wraps just in front of the hackle. If any of the hackle is unruly, wind back onto it for just a thread width or two.

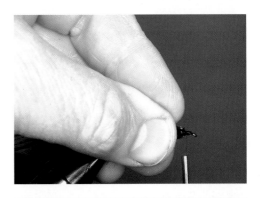

31. Flatten your thread and wrap until a smooth, neat head is formed, right up to the eye. Whip finish. Apply a drop of head cement to the thread wraps.

32. The completed fly as it should look after a little practice.

33. If you own a rotary bobbin and want to try your hand at rotary tying, the Woolly Bugger is a perfect candidate. Both the chenille and hackle can be applied with the rotary technique. Start by bringing the bobbin cradle around in front of the hook as shown. The hook should be placed in the vise so there is a minimum of up-and-down wobbling as you rotate the vise. Try to line up the shank with the axis of rotation. Some vises have adjustments for this, or you can merely move the hook up or down in the jaws as needed. Place the bobbin in the cradle—no need to tie a knot to secure it.

34. Grab the chenille and begin rotating the vise away from you—clockwise if you were sighting down from the front of the hook. Guide the chenille with your hand as it rolls forward.

35. When ready to tie off the chenille, remove the bobbin from the cradle, swivel the cradle back out of the way, and tie in the chenille as above.

36. Wind the hackle in the same way. Rotary tying is especially useful when winding hackle because you can see how it looks from all sides as you wind, not just the near side.

4

Bead-Head
Soft Hackle

IN 1995, JOE BRESSLER, LEGENDARY GUIDE AND HOMETOWN FAVORITE WON the Jackson Hole One-Fly contest with this nymph. The One-Fly is a charity event where you are only allowed a single fly each day. Needless to say, the fly patterns are carefully chosen. Joe, who grew up on the banks of the Snake while his father, the late Vern Bressler, managed some of the finest fishing lodges in Wyoming, knew he would need a fly that would catch nearly any trout in the river. He needed a pattern that could be fished deep or shallow, in fast water or slow. The morning of the competition, although Joe was reportedly nursing a hangover of world-class proportions, he had enough presence of mind to pull this fly out of his box.

This nymph is a cross between a 100-year-old Yorkshire soft-hackle wet fly pattern and the modern bead-head nymph. Beads, made from glass, brass, or tungsten, have been added to every popular nymph pattern over the past 10 years. They add sparkle and weight without having to tie lead wire under the fly or use split shot on the leader. Tungsten beads are the heaviest, brass are about 50 percent lighter, and glass beads are the lightest.

This is a pattern that works best when there are caddisflies around. If you see them in the air, on the water, or see their cases covering the bottom, a Bead-Head Soft Hackle should interest the fish. If you see no rises at all, fish it slow and deep, adding a pinch of soft weight to your leader. Fish upstream, dead drift, with a big, fuzzy yarn indicator. If you see caddis in the air and a few sporadic but splashy rises, take off the weight and indicator. Fish the fly just below the surface, across and downstream.

	MATERIAL	SUBSTITUTE
HOOK	Bead-head. Sizes 8 through 18.	2X long nymph, or short-curved nymph.
THREAD	Tan 6/0.	Any pale 6/0 or 8/0 thread, depending on hook size.
BODY	Natural Hare's Ear Plus Dubbing Brush.	Dubbed hare's ear fur or other rough fur with short guard hairs mixed in.
BEAD	Match to hook size. ⅛" Brass Bead for Size 12 fly shown here.	Tungsten bead for quicker sink rate.
HACKLE	Hungarian partridge body feather.	Any mottled gamebird feather or speckled hen chicken feather.

Using what you learn in the following fly, you can tie either regular soft-hackle wet flies or bead-head nymphs. Soft-hackle wets are usually tied with bodies of thin floss, very sparsely dubbed fur, or feather fibers like pheasant. The hackle is sparse, typically three turns of a soft body feather. The most common feather used is the Hungarian partridge, because it is widely available and has lifelike speckled markings. Hen chicken hackle can also be used. And if you hunt, ruffed grouse, woodcock, quail, and dove feathers all make wonderful soft hackles.

Bead-head nymphs are among the easiest flies you can create. If you want to turn the fly in this section into a plain old bead-head nymph, merely leave off the hackle in front of the bead, finishing the fly with the first whip finish. Bead-heads sometimes have tails and sometimes don't; the ones I use most often are merely a body with a bead. You can make the easiest bodies from pre-made materials like dubbing brushes, microchenille, or yarn. Fancier flies can be dubbed fur, peacock herl, pheasant tail, rubber bands, or nearly any material you can wind on a hook.

1. Slip a ⅛" brass bead over the hook point. You'll notice the bead has a wide opening on one side and a narrow one on the other. Slip the point of the hook into the narrow end as this makes it easier to thread the bead on the hook. Slip the bead about three-quarters of the way to the eye. Apply a drop of head cement onto the bead, letting the cement run into the hole inside the bead.

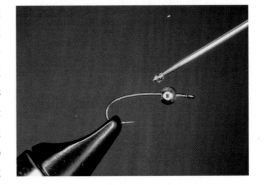

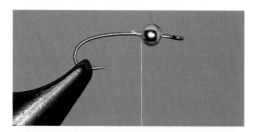

2. Start your thread immediately behind the bead.

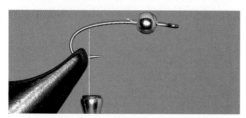

3. Wind the thread back to the end of
   the hook shank, right to where the
   bend starts to angle down.

4. Strip the fuzzy down from the base
   of a well-mottled Hungarian partridge feather. Separate six to eight
   fibers and line them up by pulling
   them at right angles to the stem of
   the feather. Pluck them all at once
   from the feather.

5. Measure the fibers against the shank.
   The fine ends should extend about
   one-half shank length beyond the
   bend. Place the fibers at a 45° horizontal angle to the shank, with the
   blunt, plucked ends facing toward
   you.

6. Take one soft turn of thread around
   the tail material without tightening.

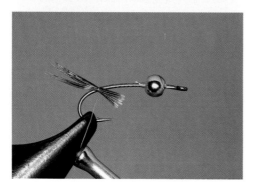

7. Start working the thread toward the eye in non-overlapping turns, applying more tension with each wrap and guiding the tail fibers parallel to the shank. They should do this naturally as you wrap. Don't let the tail fibers slip around the far side of the hook—keep them right on top of the shank.

8. Wrap the thread back to the initial tie-in point. You can make smooth turns or just spiral it back quickly. There is no need to wrap a smooth foundation of thread at this point. Pull the fur off about 1/8" of a piece of dubbing brush. There will be twisted copper wires exposed. Tie the exposed wire in with about five non-overlapping tight turns of thread. Work toward the eye. Wind the tying thread up to the bead and let it hang.

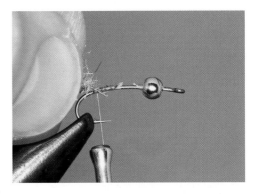

9. Wind the dubbing brush forward in turns that just touch each other. Start winding with your right hand over the top and around the far side. Transfer the material to your left hand while you bring your right hand around the bobbin. Catch the material again in your right hand.

10. Wind the dubbing brush all the way up to the bead. Tie it off tightly by holding the end of the material in your right hand while bringing the thread and bobbin behind the material with your left hand. When the bobbin reaches the far side, let it drop gently. Bring your left hand around the vise and apply tension by pulling straight down on the bobbin with your fingers locked against the spool so it does not turn. Repeat this four times.

11. Trim the dubbing brush, using the lower inside of your scissors so you do not damage the fine points when cutting the wire. If a little wire sticks up after you trim, just push it down with your finger—it's already locked in place and won't unwind.

12. Whip finish behind the bead. Let the knot dig into the dubbing so it disappears. Apply a couple drops of head cement.

13. Reattach the thread just in front of the bead.

14. Pick a Hungarian partridge feather with unbroken fibers. The fibers on each side of the stem should be about one hook shank long. Strip the fuzzy fibers from the base of both sides of the butt, or heavier end of the stem by pulling down as shown here.

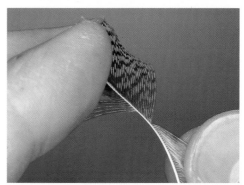

15. Grasp the feather by its very tip and stroke all of the fibers back toward the butt.

16. Trim the fibers very close to the stem about 1/8" down from the tip. These stubby fibers will help hold the delicate feather in place.

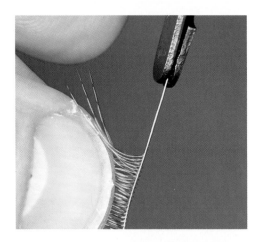

17. Tie the trimmed end of the feather just in front of the bead with five tight turns of thread. The concave or shiny side of the feather should be facing you. Work from the base of the bead toward the eye. You should not tie the feather all the way to the eye; leave a small space so you finish with a neat head. Leave the thread hanging here.

18. Grasp the heavy end of the feather with hackle pliers. Pull gently straight up and stroke all of the hackle fibers back toward the bend of the hook. Any manipulation of this delicate feather should be with a light touch as it breaks easily when winding.

19. With the hackle pliers in your right hand, begin winding the hackle away from you and around the far side. Transfer the hackle pliers briefly to your left hand on the bottom to allow your right hand to clear the bobbin. Keep steady but light pressure on the hackle pliers. Wind slightly closer to the eye with each turn. Stroke the fibers back toward the bend with your left hand as you wind. Make about three complete turns of hackle or until there is a collar of hackle fibers encircling the fly equally 360° around the hook.

20. End with the feather straight up. Tie off using the bobbin in your left hand using four tight turns. Trim the feather very close to the hook. If you trim on top like this with your thread hanging underneath the hook, you won't cut the thread accidentally.

21. Untwist your thread until it is flat, and wrap a single layer of thread over the head. If the hackle fibers don't slope back at about 45° from the vertical, wind the thread back onto the hackle very slightly while pulling them back toward the bend. Whip finish and add a drop of head cement to the head.

5

Hare's Ear
Nymph

THE HARE'S EAR FLY IS AT LEAST 500 YEARS OLD. MEDIEVAL FLIES were not dry flies or nymphs or wets—they were simply "flies" although they were fished under the surface. Sometime during the first half of the 20th Century, nymphs became the favored way of imitating subsurface insects because they are more exact replicas of subsurface life. Standard procedure was to take a wet fly and substitute a tied-down wing case for the wet fly wings, turning the old standard into a nymph. The pattern described here is the most commonly used version. The tails, wing case, and rib might be made from other materials in some variations. A bead might be added to the head of the fly. The fly might be tied on a dry-fly hook, with a short wing of CDC to create an emerger. But all of them incorporate that magic fur blend.

It is not an accident that this material has stayed popular over the centuries. There is something about the mixed natural colors of fur from the face of a rabbit that synthetic materials have yet to duplicate, based on the statistic that the Hare's Ear Nymph, with its many variations, outsells the next most popular nymph two-to-one in fly shops all over the world.

Although we don't know why this nymph is so effective, the Hare's Ear, with its spiky fibers that move in the water, looks like nothing specific but has the suggestion of many types of subsurface life. It can look like a mayfly nymph because the fibers sticking out between the gold ribs look like gills between segments of a mayfly's abdomen. The fuzzy hairs under the wing case might appear to be the struggling legs of an emerging caddisfly or mayfly. They may also approximate the whirling legs of tiny crustaceans. Stripped through the water, it might masquerade as a tiny minnow or crayfish. We hope trout pick out what they want to see and it seems to work.

You can buy pre-packaged hare's ear blends but I don't recommend them. By mixing it yourself, you'll obtain just the right color and texture and amount of guard hairs in the blend. All commercial blends are too soft and don't contain enough guard hairs because there aren't a lot of them on each ear and they are too tough to work with unless you're willing to spend the time at home.

In the following pattern, I show you two ways to dub fur. The abdomen is made from fur dubbed directly onto the thread, the best method for making a slim or tapered body. The thorax fur is dubbed onto a loop, which gives a fuzzier, wider profile. You can dub either part with either method, but this way seems to give the nymphs the best profile. Besides, you get to learn two dubbing methods on one fly.

The Hare's Ear is such an effective fly that my best suggestions on fishing techniques is to warn you when and where it may *not* work. The Hare's Ear is not a productive spring creek fly, although it is fair in smaller sizes, tied very sparse. If you're fishing weed-filled waters with slow, clear current, fish a better spring creek fly like the Pheasant Tail. It is also not the best pattern when skinny mayflies like Blue Quills or Blue-Winged Olives are hatching. Otherwise—when mayflies with meaty bodies, caddisflies, and stoneflies are around, the Hare's Ear will catch trout. Fish it

	MATERIAL	SUBSTITUTE
HOOK	2XL Nymph, sizes 8 through 20.	Bead Head.
THREAD	Black 6/0.	Any dark thread.
WEIGHT	Non-Toxic Fly Wire, .014" diameter.	Brass or tungsten bead under the wing case instead of fur thorax.
TAIL	Guard hairs from the face of a European hare.	Brown webby hackle fibers.
BODY	Dubbing mixed from fur and guard hairs of a European hare's mask, dubbed directly to waxed thread.	Dubbing from the back and belly of red or fox squirrel.
RIBBING	Fine oval gold tinsel.	Fine flat tinsel or gold wire.
WING CASE	Section from mottled turkey secondary feather.	Section from mallard primary wing quill or goose secondary wing quill.
THORAX	Same as body, dubbed on a loop.	Same as body, dubbed on a loop.

upstream, downstream, deep, or shallow. Like most nymphs, it is better fished dead-drift without added motion, but when trout are aggressive and you see splashy rises an occasional twitch or downstream swing might get their attention.

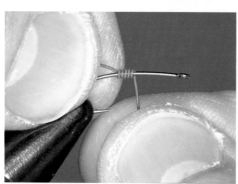

1. (A) Pull about six inches of wire from its spool. You can wind the wire with the spool cupped in the palm of your right hand or you can cut the wire from the spool first. (B) Starting at about one-quarter of the way from the bend to the eye, wind the wire in smooth adjacent turns. Cover about the middle one-half of the shank.

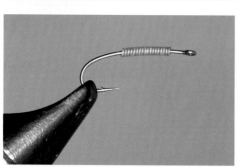

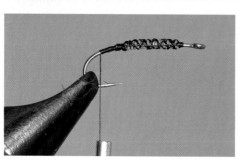

2. Don't get too close to the tail or your fly will look lumpy. And if you get too close to the eye your materials will get crowded toward the eye when you finish. Snap or cut both ends of the wire and smooth the broken ends in place with your fingernail.

3. Start your thread in front of the wire. Wind back and forth over the wire three times with the thread. Add a few drops of head cement.

4. Gather a bunch of guard hairs and fur from the lower part of a hare's mask. The ends should be relatively even and about the same diameter as the lead base already on the hook. Tie these in using either the Finger on Far Side or Pinch technique. Wind over the guard hairs, toward the eye, in smooth non-overlapping wraps. Trim the butt end of the hairs right where the wire underbody stops, creating a smooth transition. Return the tying thread to the initial tie-in point.

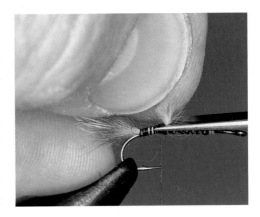

5. (A) Pull four inches of fine oval gold tinsel from the spool. With the Finger on Far Side technique, wind over one end of the tinsel toward the eye, halfway from the bend to the eye. (B) Most of the tinsel should be hanging off the end of the fly, out of the way. Bind the tinsel under to the middle of the shank and let the thread hang.

A

B

6. Pull about four inches of thread from your bobbin and coat it with wax. With practice you'll be able to dub even rough hare's ear on the pre-waxed thread as it comes from the spool, but at the beginning I think you'll find it easier with extra wax.

7. (This step is often done with large quantities before tying a number of flies). (A) Snip equal parts of fur from the soft, bottom part, the middle, and then carefully skim the short speckled hairs off the ears. Cut fur and guard hairs together, and only remove very large hairs or clumped bits of fur. (B) Mix the three bits together in a coffee grinder, or by teasing and (C) mixing back and forth with your fingers until the whole thing is a scrambled mess. Take small amounts of fur (D) and starting close to the hook, (E) squeeze wisps of fur tightly around the thread, twisting in one direction only. Do about one finger width at a time. You will use too much and you won't squeeze with enough pressure on your first attempt—guaranteed. Your first bunch, close to the hook, should be about half as big around as the underbody. The next two bunches should be even tighter and smaller in diameter, and the final bunch or two should be as wide as the first one. The whole thing should look like a greatly exaggerated, stretched hourglass.

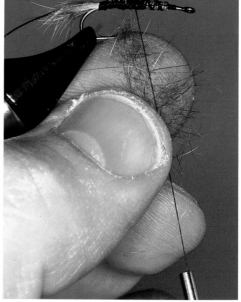

8. The reason for the subtle hourglass shape is that I prefer to double-wind my dubbed bodies. This is not a conventional technique but it makes it easier to get a tapered body, and the resulting body is more durable.

9. Start winding the dubbed thread back toward the bend in even wraps that just touch each other. If your dubbing looks any thicker than what you see here, start over. Pluck all of the dubbing off the thread and start from the beginning.

10. As you wind toward the tail, you should be winding that finer middle section. A well-tied nymph has a distinct taper from tail to thorax. If the dubbing is too thick at this point, back up, pluck some of the fur from the thread, and resume winding.

11. As soon as you reach the tail, wind back toward the eye. Try to keep that smooth taper. Putting pressure on the thread will make a smaller diameter, easing up a little will make the body thicker. By controlling the thread tension and allowing the second wrap to bury into the first you can create a smooth, life-like taper. If you don't have enough dubbing left on your thread back up and add a pinch. If you are left with too much back up and pluck some off. If you do add or subtract, make sure you twist the last part of the dubbing tightly to get a clean finish.

12. Spiral the tinsel through the body by wrapping mainly with your right hand, using the left hand to transfer the ribbing as your right goes around the bobbin. Tie off the ribbing with four very tight winds and snip the end close to the hook.

13. (A) From the top portion of the shorter side of a mottled turkey secondary quill, (B) separate a section of quill that is about one hook gape in width. Cut it from the quill. (C) Tie this in on top of the hook, right where the body ended, with the Gravity Drop with Upward Pull technique. The tip ends of the feather should be pointing back toward the bend and the shiny, concave side of the feather should be facing up.

A

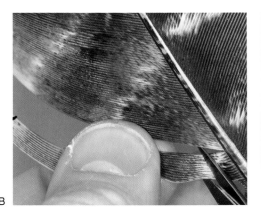

B

C

14. The feather should stay flat on top of the hook. Be careful that you avoid tying in the part of the section that was closest to the quill, as that part of the feather will split easily when you tie it in. If the feather slips to the far side, try to roll it back to the top, otherwise cut a new section of feather and try again.

15. Bind the ends of the quill under, winding about half way to the eye. Snip the ends of the quill.

16. Pull eight inches of thread from your bobbin, loop it around your finger, and return the bobbin to the hook. Make a couple of winds around the hook to secure the loop. Wind the thread forward to a point that is about four turns of thread from the eye.

17. Place the ends of the loop in the hooks of a dubbing twister, or hang a pair of hackle pliers on the closed end of the loop. Wax both sides of the loop.

18. Push up slightly with the dubbing tool or hackle pliers to open the loop. Place a fairly large, loose clump of hare's ear fur inside the loop, as close to the hook as possible.

19. Close the loop by letting the tool or the hackle pliers drop.

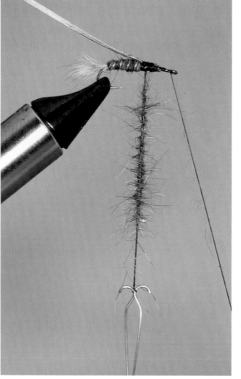

20. Spin the tool or hackle pliers in a counterclockwise direction (looking at it from above the hook). Keep spinning until all of the fur is trapped between the thread and a fuzzy chenille is formed.

21. Wind the fur chenille forward to the eye with your right hand, stroking the long fibers back at each wrap with your left hand.

22. At a point that is well clear of the eye (between $\frac{1}{16}$ and $\frac{1}{8}$ inch behind the eye), tie off the fur chenille with your tying thread using about five very tight wraps. Trim the ends very close to the shank.

23. Wind back over the fur a bit to allow plenty of room to tie in the wing case without crowding the eye.

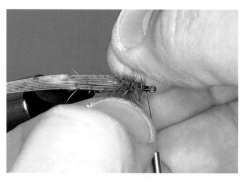

24. At this point, I like to pull fibers straight out from the thorax with my fingers to get an impression of legs under the wing case.

25. Pull the wing case straight over the eye and tie it in with the Gravity Drop with Upward Pull. After the first wrap, pull up and back slightly on the wing case to make sure it has not gotten too close to the eye.

A

26. (A) Make four very tight turns over the wing case, and again pulling up and back on it, trim the ends of the feather very close to the hook. (B) Flatten your thread and wrap over the head until the wing case fibers are completely covered. Whip finish. At this point inspect your fly to make sure there is enough fur sticking out from the thorax. (C) If it doesn't look like this, gently pick out some fur with your dubbing needle. Add a drop of cement to the head windings.

B

C

6

Adams

For as long as I have been with the Orvis Company, 24 years as I'm writing this, the Size 14 Adams was the most popular fly, year after year. Not just the most popular *dry* fly—more of these were sold than any pattern of any type. That's quite an accomplishment for a fly originally designed to imitate a pesky land-bred insect that hardly ever gets into the water.

The Adams was developed in the 1930s by Michigan angler Len Halliday as a deer fly imitation for the Boardman River. I've never fished the Boardman, but unless it is unlike any other trout stream in the world deer flies are probably not prime trout food. Deer flies hatch in dry soil in coniferous forests and mate over land, and the only deer flies I have ever seen in a trout stream are ones I swatted from around my head, gleefully crunched between my fingers, and tossed into the water.

I am having fun at the expense of one of the most devilishly productive dry flies ever invented. It is a traditional dry fly with classic lines, which means it does not look much like a mayfly. Yet during mayfly hatches, this gray-bodied, brown-and-black-and-white-winged fly catches trout when pink-bodied, gray-winged Hendricksons are on the water. The Adams is known as a deadly fly during caddis hatches, yet it has upright wings and tails—appendages that adult caddis don't sprout. In smaller sizes, it fools trout during Blue-Winged Olive and midge hatches.

Why does it work? We don't know and probably never will. Trout may not see flies in their entirety and may just pick out a certain pattern in the naturals and our imitations. Just use the Adams on faith, enjoy the fun of casting to rising trout, and delight in using a traditional pattern.

	MATERIAL	SUBSTITUTE
HOOK	Extra-Fine Dry Fly, sizes 10 through 14. Bigeye Dry sizes 16 to 24.	None.
THREAD	Black, 8/0 or 10/0.	White.
TAIL	Mixed brown and grizzly hackle fibers.	Just brown or just grizzly hackle fibers.
BODY	Dubbed muskrat fur.	Medium gray packaged dubbing.
WINGS	Hen grizzly hackle tips.	Round hackle tips from grizzly rooster or saddle hackles.
HACKLE	Mixed brown and grizzly.	Ginger grizzly or cree hackle.

A few notes on tying this pattern: It's a traditional dry-fly pattern and if you master this one, you'll also be able to tie the famous Catskill dries like the Hendrickson and Light Cahill. If you have trouble mixing the tails, don't. It's just as effective with either brown or grizzly tails. I prefer using natural muskrat because it's easy to dub, looks translucent, and floats well; you can use a gray packaged dubbing if you like. If you tie these smaller than Size 18 (the Adams makes a terrific adult midge imitation), just leave off the wings. Finally, try the Adams as a parachute, substituting white calf body hair for the grizzly hackle tips, winding the hackles around the base of the wing.

1. Attach the thread in the middle of the shank and wind back to the bend in smooth wraps. Stop just before the bend starts to slope below the horizontal. Search the side of a grizzly hackle cape for a spade feather that has firm, glossy fibers. These will always be found about halfway up the cape on each side.

2. This may sound silly, but it enables you to pluck tail fibers from a feather without removing the feather from the cape: Place the cape, skin side down, against your chest. Pull the selected feather out to the side with thumb and forefinger of your right hand. Brace the pinkie of your right hand at the bottom of the feather, at the far side of the stem. With thumb and middle finger of your left hand, find about a dozen stiff fibers, pull them together at right angles to the stem, and pluck them all at once.

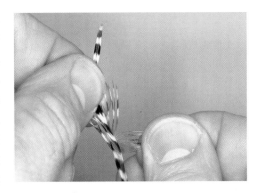

3. You should have a nice bunch of tail fibers, all lined up. Set these down gently where they won't get knocked around.

4. Repeat the procedure with a bunch of brown hackle fibers. Transfer these to your right hand so the tips are sticking out beyond the end of your thumb and forefinger. Now pick up the grizzly fibers and try to line up their ends with the brown ones. If you have trouble, place them in a small stacker.

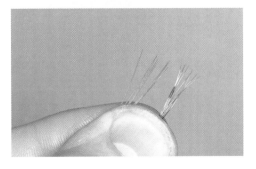

5. Measure the tails, using the shank as a guide. They should be about one shank length the tips of your fingers. If the length extending beyond them is too short, pull the fibers out. If they are too long, choke up a bit with your fingertips.

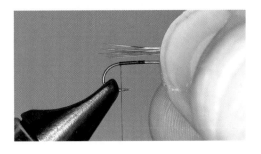

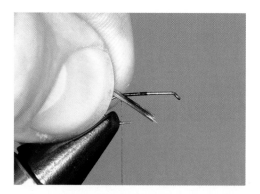

6. Carefully transfer the fibers to your left hand, pinching them at the same spot you just measured. Line them up at a 45° horizontal with the shank, with the butts pointing toward you.

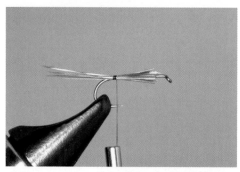

7. Make one fairly loose wrap as you start to angle the fibers so they line up with the shank.

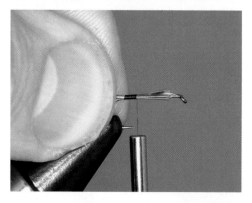

8. Make three more wraps toward the eye with increasing tension until they line up perfectly. If they start to roll to the far side, roll them back.

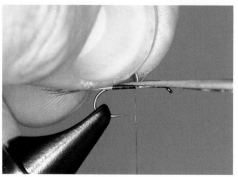

9. Wrap the thread in smooth wraps toward the eye until you get to the middle of the shank. Trim the butts of the tail fibers. Wrap the thread forward to about four thread widths short of the eye, then back toward the bend to a point that is one-quarter shank length behind the eye. This forms a thread foundation for the wings.

10. Select two hen grizzly hackles that are slightly less than one hook gap in width. They will be more evenly matched if you pluck them from the same place on the cape.

11. Place them along the shank and measure one shank length down from the tip.

12. Beyond this point, stroke the fibers down toward the stem so they stand at right angles to it.

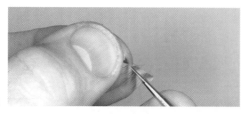

A

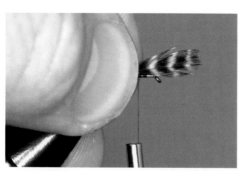

B

13. (A) With the point of your scissors, trim the hackle fibers very close to both sides of the stem so there is fine stubble (B) on either side of it.

14. With your left hand, line the point between the trimmed and untrimmed hackle stem right over the top of where the thread is hanging. The tips of the hackles should be pointing out over the eye.

15. Tie in the hackle tips with three wraps, using the Pinch technique.

16. Flatten the thread and wrap back toward the bend over the butts of the hackles until you meet the point where you trimmed the tails. Trim the butts here.

17. Wrap the thread forward and right in front of the wings. Pull the wings straight up with your left hand. Twist the thread if it is not already twisted and wind about four turns right up against the base of the wings.

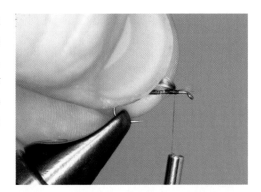

18. The wings should now be sticking straight up. If not, make two more wraps in front of the wings.

19. Push down gently on the wings to divide them.

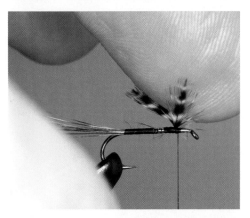

20. Grab the near wing with your left hand.

21. Bring the thread up and cross it between the wings on top of the shank.

22. Continue winding the thread on the far side and under the shank, directly behind the far wing. Grab the far wing with your left hand.

23. Bring the thread up behind the near wing and cross the shank between the wings, ending immediately in front of the far wing. These last four steps are called a figure-8 wind and are essential steps in dividing upright dry-fly wings.

24. Repeat the figure-8 wind and make two more turns immediately in front of the wings. Trim any hackle fibers that might have gotten bound under.

25. From the side, the wings should be evenly matched and cocked about 30° below the vertical. If they aren't, the fly will be out of balance and will twist your tippet.

26. Prepare some muskrat dubbing. (A) Pull a bunch of fur from the hide, about a little finger width for each fly you plan to tie. (B) Cut it as close to the hide as possible. Pinch the bunch of fur in the middle with one hand. (C) Carefully pull the long brown guard hairs out of the bunch. You should be left with a soft, fuzzy pinch of fur. (D) Tease the fur back and forth between your fingers until all the fibers are swirled around and confused.

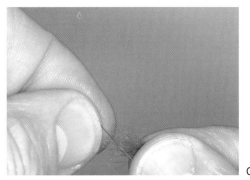

27. Tease a small bunch of fur from the ball. The fur should be as fine and loose as you see here.

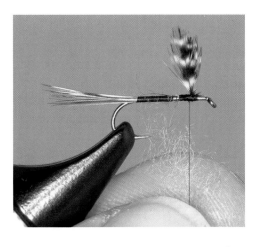

28. Using small amounts of fur and lots of pressure, roll the fur onto the thread with your fingers. Roll in one direction only. Dub fur over about four inches of thread, in a very slight and elongated hourglass shape, with the thinnest diameter of dubbing in the middle.

29. You will have a short length of thread that is not dubbed. Use this to wrap back to a point just ahead of the midpoint of the hook. Wrap here until the dubbing first touches the shank.

30. Wrap back to the tail, being careful not to overlap the dubbing at the tail. Hopefully you've calculated correctly and the middle point of your dubbing, the thinnest place, will end up at the tail. If not, you can sometimes back up a bit or spiral forward. Because of this double layer of dubbing, you get more margin for error. Wind the dubbing back toward the wings, striving for a slight taper. If you get a lump, either put more pressure on the thread or don't overlap so much. If you get a gap in the dubbing, dally there for a wrap or loosen up on your thread pressure to get a slightly bigger diameter.

31. Add a pinch of dubbing if needed, or pluck some off if you have too much. You should end up well behind the wings, just forward of the midpoint of the hook, so you have room to wind hackle behind the wings.

32. Select one brown and one grizzly hackle with fibers that are one and one-half to twice the gap in length. When tying a dry fly with two hackles from the same neck, you always take both hackles from the same spot on the cape so they are evenly matched. Because you must take hackles from two different capes, pay even more attention to how close the fibers are in length, otherwise your fly will look sloppy. I like to fan them together around the hook before tying in to make sure they match. Strip the bottoms of the hackles so any webby fibers are removed. Place them both together so the bottoms of their fibers line up and the shiny (convex) side of one is against the dull (concave) side of the other. Tie the hackles in together, immediately in front of the dubbed body, with their dull sides facing up or toward you. Make sure you leave a bit of bare stem behind the tie-in point. The stems can extend between the wings if they are long. Wind forward in smooth, tight turns to just behind the wings.

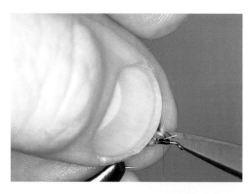

33. Trim the stems in the middle of the wing crotch by lifting the stems gently and carefully placing the tips of your scissors between them.

34. Wind the thread forward to about four thread widths short of the eye.

35. Grab the top hackle, or the one facing you (could be either color, the order in which you tie them in is not important) with your right fingertips or hackle pliers. It should roll on its side so the dull side of the hackle is now facing forward. If not, twist it slightly or wrap backwards for one revolution until it behaves.

36. Wind this first hackle flush to the end of the dubbed body but not on top of it. You should always be winding toward the eye. You'll probably make one revolution before the hackle fibers come into play; this is good as it lets you line things up.

37. Wind up to the base of the wings with even wraps that don't quite touch. With some hackles this might be two turns, with others it could be three or four.

38. Grasp the wings in your left hand and pull them back slightly. Make a wind of hackle immediately in front of the wings.

39. Continue to wrap forward, about two more turns, until the hackle is where the thread was left hanging.

40. Hold the hackle on top of the shank and tie it in with three very tight wraps.

41. Trim the hackle carefully with the point of your scissors.

42. Go back to the other hackle and wind in the same manner. This one will have to wind its way between the first, so try to place each wrap beside the stem of the first. You can also wiggle it back and forth a bit as you wind.

43. As you come in front of the wings, pull them back for a moment as you did with the first hackle.

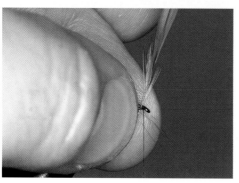

44. On the very last wind, grasp all the other fibers by sweeping your left thumb and forefinger from the eye back until you capture them all. Make one final turn with the second hackle right in front of your fingers, which should help keep all of the other fibers out of the hook eye.

45. Flatten your thread, wrap until all the hackle stems are covered (but no more than a half-dozen wraps), whip finish, and apply a drop of head cement.

7

Letort
Hopper

F ISHING IN MIDSUMMER WITHOUT A HOPPER PATTERN IN YOUR BOX IS like playing cards without a full deck. The combination of a trout stream, a grass meadow, and a gust of wind serves up the easiest dry-fly fishing (and sometimes the biggest trout) of the season. You'll be warned by the soft castanet crackling of their wings in the brush; the trout already know. Trout eat hopper artificials as eagerly as they do naturals because your fly does what a hopper is supposed to do—it plops onto the water with no semblance of grace, unlike the delicate aquatic insects that come from beneath the surface.

The best place to fish this hopper is right up against the bank. Not a foot but an inch from the bank as large trout will lie in open, shallow water during hopper season, especially if there is deeper water or a big log close at hand. Cast to a likely spot as close to the bank as you can, or actually up on the bank, twitching the fly into the water quickly, before the current drags your line. If nothing happens, try casts increasingly farther from shore. If you still don't have any luck and you haven't disturbed the water with a clumsy cast, try twitching the fly a fraction every few inches, as it drifts downstream. And if all else fails, try a steady retrieve. Don't overlook tiny side channels as trout will move into them to eat hoppers, and most are overlooked by fishermen and drift boats.

Complicated hopper patterns are fun to tie and look great in your box. However, I've had my best luck with an older, simpler pattern, developed by the great Pennsylvania limestone stream expert Ed Schenk in the 1950s. The Letort Hopper is clean, straightforward, easy to tie, and easy to see on the water. In contrast, some

	MATERIAL	SUBSTITUTE
HOOK	2 XL Dry Fly, sizes 6 through 14.	Extra Fine Dry Fly.
THREAD	White or yellow, Size 6/0.	
BODY	Yellow fuzzy yarn or dubbed fur.	Tan or green yarn.
WING	Mottled turkey secondary wing quill section, strengthened with acrylic sealer and trimmed to shape.	Synthetic, imitation turkey feather.
HEAD AND COLLAR	Fine whitetail deer.	Coastal deer.

of the fancier imitations float too low in the water and so it's difficult to keep sight of your fly, an important consideration because, despite the size of a grasshopper, a large brown trout can eat one while barely wrinkling the surface. This pattern can also be tied down to a Size 14, great for the first part of hopper season when the tiny nymph hoppers are just emerging.

This pattern also teaches you an important tying technique, the deer hair head. Put a collar on the bottom of the hook as well as on the top and you've mastered the head of the famous Muddler Minnow. Spin deer hair on the entire shank as you'll do for the forward part of the head on this fly and you'll be able to make a Bomber salmon dry fly or a bass bug.

After you've mastered this one, have some fun making hoppers with knotted legs, foam bodies, and golden pheasant tippet underwings. But keep those on the top layer of your fly box for show. Underneath, make sure you have Letort Hoppers in size 6 through 14.

1. Attach thread to the hook about one-third of the way back from the eye. Wrap back to where the bend starts, then forward to your starting point. The idea here is to get a thread base so that when you wind the dubbing it has something to grip; it doesn't matter if the thread is twisted or flat; in fact don't even worry about neatness.

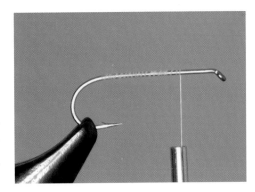

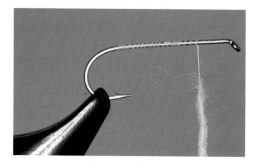

2. Dub any soft yellow fur or synthetic dubbing on the thread. Taper is not as important in this pattern, but a slight "waist" in the middle of the dubbing helps prevent a lump at the bend. The dubbing applied can be thicker than you would dub for a mayfly imitation.

3. Wind dubbing back to the bend in slightly overlapping turns. To thicken the dubbing, overlap more and ease off on thread tension. To thin the dubbing, especially at the bend, space out the wraps a bit more and put more tension on the thread.

4. Wind dubbing back to the starting point. Add or remove small amounts of dubbing as needed toward the end. Wind bare thread back onto the dubbing a few turns to form a base for the wing.

5. Snip a section from the middle of a mottled turkey secondary wing quill. It's easier if you spray the feather with fixative and let it dry first. The section should be about three-quarter hook gaps wide.

6. Round the tip end of the feather section with your scissors.

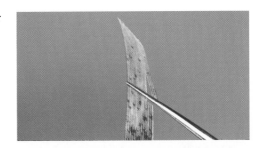

7. The trimmed feather should look like this. Make sure the feather you started with was long enough so you won't be tying over the lower one-third of the feather (the part closest to the quill), as it will split as soon as you put any tension on the thread.

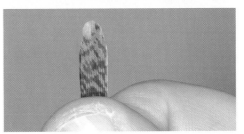

8. Place the turkey feather flat over the top of the shank, concave side down. It should extend about one-quarter shank length beyond the bend. Hold it in place with your left index finger.

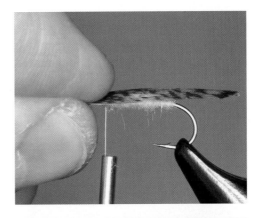

9. Bring one wrap of thread over the top of the feather with no tension—the Gravity Drop Method. Lift your finger to let the thread in but put it back in place as soon as the thread passes over the wing. Let the bobbin's weight apply the pressure. Make a second wrap the same way, then push down with your left fingertip while pulling down with the bobbin.

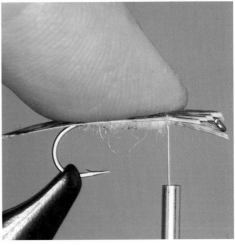

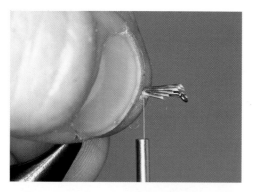

10. Now grasp the base of the wing with your left thumb and forefinger while making about six tight wraps, working slightly forward with each wrap.

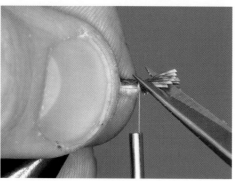

11. Trim the butt of the wing , leaving a short stub, but keeping it well clear of the eye. Wrap about six more turns over the wing stubs. You should still be left with about one-eighth bare shank just behind the eye.

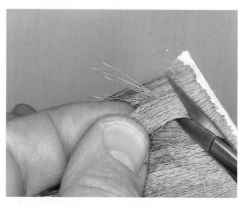

12. Snip a bunch of fine deer hair with even tips from the hide. It should be about one hook gap in diameter.

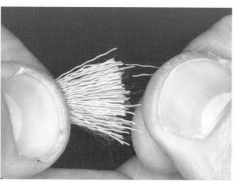

13. Clean the fuzz and short hairs from the butt end of the hair by holding the fine, untrimmed ends in your left thumb and forefinger, pulling the fuzz out with your right finger-tips.

14. Place the hair in a stacker, fine ends down, and rap sharply about four times.

15. Hold the stacker horizontally, slowly remove the tube, and grab the bunch of hair carefully by its tips with your left hand. Transfer the hair to your right hand, so you are holding the butts of the hair in your right thumb and forefinger.

16. Hold the hair over the place where you tied in the wing. The tips should extend about halfway down the wing—just short of the hook bend.

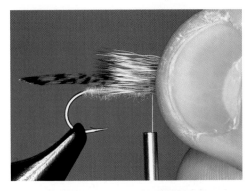

17. Pinch the hair in the same spot with your left thumb and forefinger and remove your right hand.

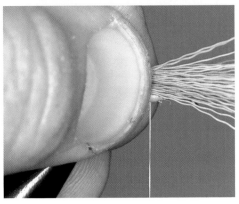

18. Putting lateral pressure on the hair with your left fingertips, keep the hair on top of the shank while working a wrap of thread between your fingertips. Pull straight down with the thread while pinching the hair. Repeat the pinch method about six times, making firm wraps.

19. When you remove your fingers, the fly should look like this—a neat collar of fine hair pointing back, and a mess of flared hair in front. Check to make sure that the collar is mostly on top of the shank.

20. Reach in front of the tying thread. Place your thumb and forefinger against the shank and push the flared hair butts back toward the wing with your fingernails. Wiggle the hair around slightly, until it is fairly evenly distributed, 360° around the shank.

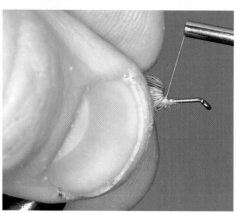

21. Grab the hair butts with your left thumb and forefinger and pull them back over the wing, exposing the shank in front of the wing and collar. Wrap enough tight turns of thread immediately in front of the hair so the butts stand 90° to the shank when you release them.

22. Cut another bunch of hair, slightly bigger than the first. Trim off the tips so that when you trim the head you can tell the collar from the rest of the deer hair head and won't trim any of the collar by mistake.

23. Hold this bunch of hair in the middle with your left fingertips. The length of this bunch does not matter.

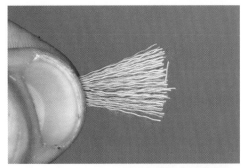

24. Place the middle of this hair on top of the shank, right over the bare shank you have been saving and hopefully avoiding with your thread. Deer hair spins okay over a thread-covered shank, but better over a bare shank. Take one loose turn of thread over the hair. Don't put any tension on the thread.

25. Take a second turn of thread in the exact same spot. This time, apply slight tension to the hair and begin releasing your grip on the hair.

26. Take a third wrap, this time applying full tension with the bobbin with your right hand and letting go of the hair with your left. The hair will flare and spin around the hook. Take about four more tight turns of thread in the same place, letting the hair spin all around the hook. If it doesn't cover the top, bottom, and both sides of the shank evenly, work it around with your fingers.

27. Push the deer hair back toward the wing by sliding your fingernails back along the shank.

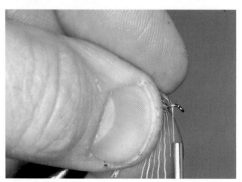

28. Pull all of the hair back out of the way. Make about six tight wraps immediately in front of the hair, then wrap a few more to form the head.

29. Whip finish, being careful not to catch any deer hair fibers.

30. You can trim the deer hair head in the vise or in your hand. A rotary vise makes trimming easy while still keeping the fly in the vise. Turn the fly upside-down and trim almost all of the hair from the bottom of the fly. If you keep the scissors parallel to the shank and use the body as a guide you won't cut into the hair windings by mistake.

31. Turn the fly right-side up and trim the top of the head. Cut upward at about a 30° angle, using the eye and the collar as guides.

32. The head should now look like this, ready to trim the sides.

33. Trim first one side, then the next. As on the bottom, trim fairly close to the head, using the shank and body as guides.

A

B

34. You will probably be left with some long hairs still on top of the head. You can trim these by placing your scissors sideways against the collar, sliding them down toward the head and opening them at the same time. The long butt hairs should get caught in your scissors, where they can be snipped out of the way without cutting into the collar.

35. (A) Inspect the head from all angles to make sure it is trimmed evenly. (B) Neat deer hair heads don't matter to the fish but you might care. Apply two drops of deep-penetrating head cement to the thread head, letting one drop seep back into the base of the deer hair from the thread.

8

Chartreuse
Clouser Minnow

I'M SHOWING THIS FLY AS A SALTWATER PATTERN, TIED ON A saltwater hook, but don't ignore it for freshwater fishing. Lefty Kreh has caught over 70 different species of fish on this fly, from Alaska to Australia. The original pattern, developed by Bob Clouser for smallmouth bass in the Susquehanna River, was designed to keep moving through the water no matter what the angler was doing. The rationale is that baitfish, when pursued by bigger fish, don't stop to look at the scenery. When this fly hits the water it sinks quickly. When you start a retrieve, it swims through the water, but if you stop moving the fly, it keeps moving as it sinks deeper. The only time it stops is when it's lying on the bottom or grabbed by a fish.

Although the Clouser is a superb baitfish imitation, I don't believe its usefulness stops there. Tied with sparse, translucent materials it becomes a credible facsimile of a shrimp. Tied shorter and fuller, it may remind gamefish of a crab—I don't know any reason a striper or bonefish would inhale a fly that has stopped moving and is resting on the bottom like a frightened crab, and I've hooked many fish this way.

I've been surprised by the number of saltwater fisheries where a chartreuse-and-white Clouser is the most popular fly. From New England stripers to North Carolina Spanish mackerel to Gulf Coast sea trout, the fly most anglers start with is a Chartreuse Clouser. In sizes 4 and 6, it has even become a top bonefish fly in the Florida Keys and the Bahamas.

In open water, particularly over breaking fish, just cast a Clouser as far as you can and strip it back with a steady retrieve. Often, a very fast retrieve will interest fish that ignore a slower moving fly. It's smart to experiment with depths—probably the best line for fishing Clousers is an intermediate, but there will be times when the fly must run deeper, so full-sinking lines might be needed. Although a floating line is not the best line to use with a Clouser, an advantage when using this fly is that you can switch from a popper to a Clouser and, letting the Clouser sink before you retrieve, get a wide range of depths without changing lines.

In currents, along jetties, or in water flowing swiftly through an estuary, a deadly technique is to cast up-current to let the fly sink, then pump the rod with six-inch twitches as the fly swings around, without retrieving any line. You can cover a lot of water this way and your fly looks like a crippled baitfish tumbling in the current.

In shallow flats, a steady retrieve may work, especially if you think the fish are eating baitfish. But if you see wakes or tails or just cruising fish, try imitating a small crustacean: Cast well ahead of the fish's suspected path and let the fly sink to the bottom. When the fish gets within four or five feet of the fly, make it hop once by giving the line one short strip. Often, the fish will sweep over and inhale the fly without any further movement on your part, but if not, try a series of short hops along the bottom. You can even do this when fish aren't visible, although it takes a pretty good leap of faith. Cast out, let the fly sink, and use short strips punctuated by long pauses—five or ten seconds between strips.

Although the chartreuse-and-white variation of the Clouser described here is the most popular, they are tied in a wide variety of colors, and you can use synthetic hair as well as other natural hairs like squirrel or calf tail. Flies can be tailored

	MATERIAL	SUBSTITUTE
HOOK	Pre-Sharpened Saltwater, sizes 1/0 through 8.	Regular stainless hook.
THREAD	White 3/0.	Black.
EYES	Weighted Dumbbell Eyes, prepainted.	Machined brass eyes with recess on ends; painted or glued-on eyes.
BELLY	White bucktail.	White Ultra Hair; or any other color Ultra Hair or bucktail.
LATERAL LINE	Pearl Krystal Flash.	Any color Krystal Flash or Flashabou.
BACK	Chartreuse bucktail.	Chartreuse Ultra Hair; or any other color Ultra Hair or Bucktail.

to fishing conditions as well. For baitfish imitations in most waters, use very small amounts of hair and tie them long, about twice as long as the shank. Keep the eyes relatively small. For patterns used on the flats where fish may be eating crustaceans, keep the flies sparse but shorten the hair to about one and one-half shank lengths. For surf fishing, particularly for striped bass, I like to follow the great surf guide Tony Stetzko and tie them very full, with big, heavy eyes.

A note of caution when using Clousers with heavy eyes in the windy surf: A gust of wind that blows your fly into the fragile tip of a graphite rod can fracture the graphite, and the only remedy for this is a new tip from the manufacturer. And the same Clouser moving at 120 mph, hitting the back of your head, can make you see stars for a few minutes.

1. Attach your thread to the shank near the front of the fly. Wind back and forth over the front one-third of the shank until you have about three layers of thread.

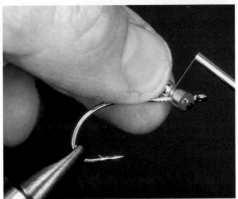

2. Hold a pair of dumbbell eyes across the shank, about one-quarter shank length behind the eye.

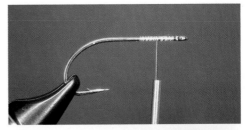

3. Wrap the thread diagonally between the eyes, from behind the eyes to the front and around the shank, with at least a dozen very firm wraps.

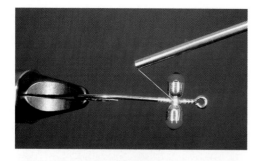

4. Straighten the eyes with your fingers until they are at a 90° angle to the shank. Wrap another dozen turns in the opposite direction, from in front of the eyes to behind them and around the shank. Keep straightening the eyes with your finger.

5. Take about eight very tight turns of thread between the eyes and the shank in a circular fashion. This locks in the diagonal turns you made previously.

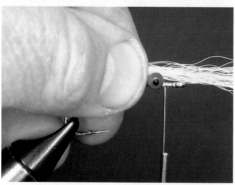

6. Cut a bunch of white bucktail that is about half the hook gap in diameter when flattened into a fan. Measure the bucktail against the shank. It should be two to two-and-one-half shank lengths from the tie-in point. Make sure the thread is just in front of the eyes and hold the bucktail right above the eyes.

7. Make about six firm wraps of thread over the bucktail. Because the eyes get in the way, you can't do a true Pinch Wrap, so if the bucktail rolls to the far side, straighten it with your fingers after tying it in.

8. Pull the bucktail toward the bend, from behind the eyes.

9. Cross the thread behind the eyes and make another six firm wraps over the hair.

10. The bucktail should be in line with the shank as shown. If not, work it into place with your fingers.

11. Bring the thread back in front of the eyes and trim the bucktail close to the shank by lifting it up at about a 45° angle.

12. Make firm wraps over the butt ends of the bucktail, working toward the eye of the hook and then back to get a slight taper.

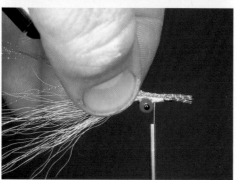

13. Turn the hook upside-down in the vise, or if you have a rotary vise, rotate the jaws 180°. Grab about a dozen strands of Krystal Flash and tie it in immediately in front of the eyes with five or six turns of thread.

14. Trim the Krystal Flash the same way you did the bucktail.

15. Cut a bunch of chartreuse bucktail the same diameter as the white bucktail. Line it up with the white hair so that it is equal in length or slightly longer.

16. Tie in the bucktail with eight very tight wraps. Notice that it slipped to the far side because I couldn't get my fingers in there to make a proper pinch wrap.

17. Grasp the bucktail over the eyes with your left hand and use your right hand to roll it back on top of the shank. Make sure it is centered on top of the shank here in the front, but don't worry if the back end of the bucktail is not centered over the point of the hook at this point. As long as it is lined up over the eyes, you can distribute it around the bend of the hook later.

18. Trim the chartreuse bucktail in the same manner.

19. Wind the butts of the hair under and form a tapered head by winding the thread back and forth from the hook eye to the dumbbell eyes. Whip finish and trim your thread.

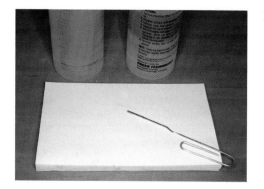

20. I feel a Clouser is a better fly if the head is expoxied. The hair won't pull out and the eyes won't move off-center—if they do, the fly may not swim right and you will sacrifice strikes. Go to your local hardware store and get two-part, 30-minute epoxy, paper clips and Post-Its. You'll also need a battery-operated fly turner unless you want to baby-sit each fly by turning it in the vise every ten seconds for about fifteen minutes. You can use five-minute epoxy and shorten the set-up time to about three minutes, but it's trickier to use.

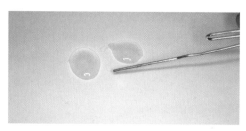

21. Place two equal globs of hardener and resin on the Post-It.

22. Mix the epoxy thoroughly until it is of a single consistency. Don't stir too hard or you'll introduce air bubbles. (I used to use toothpicks for mixing and applying epoxy until 14-year-old Luca Adelphio of Washington, D.C., warned me that the toothpicks would yellow the epoxy.)

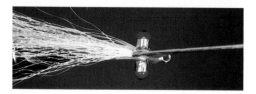

23. Work some epoxy into the thread and hair between the eyes, and run just a bit onto the hair behind the eyes.

24. Carefully coat the head of the fly, making sure you get all sides. A rotary vise makes this easy. If you get any epoxy in the hook eye, remove it now with a toothpick or by drawing a feather through the eye. If it hardens, you'll have to drill it out!

25. Place the hook in a rotating fly drier. The 30-minute epoxy will actually set up in 15 minutes or less, but it will be very tacky for a few hours. Heat speeds the process; humidity hinders it. If you are in a hurry or the weather is humid, place a desk lamp about six inches from the drier. Avoid touching the fly for six hours. When you're done, the head will be nearly indestructible and will look like this.

26. Now you can preen the hair and distribute it equally around the hook bend.

27. The completed Clouser Minnow.

28. A Clouser with eyes hand-painted on the ends of plain dumbbell eyes.

29. A Clouser with doll eyes attached to plain dumbbell eyes with head cement, then epoxied over the top for durability.